JESUS

D1297328

THE
ULTIMATE
REALITY

BOB EMERY

BENCH PRESS PUBLISHING

Scripture taken from the *New American Standard Bible*, © 1960, 1962, 1963, 1968, 1971, 1972, 1973, 1975, 1977, 1995 by The Lockman Foundation. Used by permission. (www.Lockman.org)

Scripture quotations marked HCSB are taken from the *Holman Christian Standard Bible*. Used by Permission. HCSB ©1999, 2000, 2002, 2003, 2009 Holman Bible Publishers. Holman Christian Standard Bible, Holman CSB, and HCSB are federally registered trademarks of Holman Bible Publishers.

Scripture quotations marked TPT are from *The Passion Translation*. © 2017, 2018 by Passion & Fire Ministries, Inc. Used by permission. All rights reserved. ThePassionTranslation.com.

Scripture quotations marked (NIV) are taken from the *Holy Bible, New International Version*, NIV. © 1973, 1978, 1984, 2011 by Biblica, Inc™. Used by permission of Zondervan. All rights reserved worldwide. www.zondervan. com. The "NIV" and "New International Version" are trademarks registered in the United States Patent and Trademark Office by Biblica, Inc™.

Scripture taken from *The Source: With Extensive Notes on Greek Word Meaning.* © 2004 by Ann Nyland. Used by permission of Smith and Stirling Publishers. All rights reserved.

ISBN 978-0-9976444-1-8

Front Cover imagery courtesy of Shutterstock by Elena Akimova, Anassia Art, Saysio, Komleva, and Sarah O'Neal
Cover Design and Book Layout Design by Sarah O'Neal | Eve Custom Artwork

Printed in the United States of America

This book is available on Amazon.com

BenchPress Publishing

P.O. Box 5846 | Charlottesville, VA 22905

CONTENTS

DEDICATION

THIS BOOK IS DEDICATED TO MY FAMILY: TO SANDRA, THE BEAUTIFUL WOMAN THAT GOD GAVE TO ME AS MY BRIDE FIFTY YEARS AGO, AND WHO IS STILL AS BEAUTIFUL TODAY, AND EVEN MORE SO IN GODLY CHARACTER AND LOVE FOR THE LORD. WE GROW MORE THANKFUL EACH PASSING DAY FOR ALL THAT THE LORD HAS GIVEN US, ESPECIALLY FOR OUR TWO PRICELESS DAUGHTERS, ERICKA AND KATIE, THEIR FABULOUS HUSBANDS, JASON AND STEVE, AND OUR PRECIOUS GRANDKIDS— ISAAC, NADINE, NATE, AND GRACE, WHO WE LOVE AND ADORE SO MUCH.

YOU WILL KNOW THE TRUTH
and the truth will set you free.

—Jesus

JOHN 8:32

JESUS: THE ULTIMATE REALITY

THIS BOOK IS FOR ALL TRUTH-SEEKERS.

I began writing this book with new followers of Jesus in mind, because I wanted to write something that would get them off to a good start in following him. That still remains the focus. However, this would also be a good book for agnostics, skeptics, and atheists, as well as those who already consider themselves Christians. Why? Because it addresses the universal question that all people—regardless of their race, religion, education, or philosophical orientation—have a deep heart-cry to discover. That is: *what is Truth?*

We could begin our search for the answer to this question by looking at what the great philosophers had to say about it, beginning with the ancients—men like Aristotle, Socrates, and Plato, who spent the majority of their lives searching for truths and then attempting to explain them in ways that people could understand. Or we could look to more modern thinkers: philosophers, poets, successful business CEOs, or educators. But for me, that's not the best place to start.

I prefer to go to the source: *the best place to start is with Jesus.*

No one with intellectual honesty would question Jesus' existence. Not only did those who knew him or were close to him—his earliest followers and disciples—write about him, but secular historians living at the time, such as Josephus, wrote about him as well.

There is no one in human history that has had the influence that Jesus of Nazareth has had. He was no ordinary human being. Jesus claimed that he came from God, that he pre-existed with God, and that he was God. These are some extraordinary claims. Plus his early disciples and 500 other witnesses attest to seeing him after he was raised from the dead, three days after he was crucified. At a minimum, anyone with these credentials merits at least a fair hearing when it comes to listening to what he has to say regarding truth.

Jesus said, *"I am the way, the truth, and the life; no one comes to the Father [God] but through me"* (John 14:6).

Jesus didn't say that he *knew* the truth, but that he *was* the truth.

That is why anyone with a serious curiosity to discover what truth is, will ultimately end up considering Jesus. Accept him or reject him, but a quest for truth without a thorough investigation of Jesus is not an honest one.

A thorny part of this discussion is coming to an agreement on what the word "truth" means. Truth is kind of a nebulous word. It's hard to define and can get away from you—sort of like squeezing a handful of Jell-O.

I recently did a Google search for a definition of truth, and here's what I came up with: the quality or state of being true. Now that's a BIG help, isn't it?

However, by going back to the Bible and seeing how New Testament writers dealt with the word truth in relation to Jesus is quite helpful. The book that provides the most in-depth and concentrated look at this is the Book of John.

The New Testament was written in Greek. The Greek word that John used that translates into the English word "truth" is aletheia. The literal meaning is "the state of not being hidden; the state of being evident." It also means factuality or reality.

When John described Jesus as being "full of truth," what John was saying was: Jesus was the real deal. In fact, Jesus is reality itself. This topic is further developed in John's Gospel, which we'll be looking at in this book. So don't worry if that definition is a little confusing at present; we'll be returning to it again and again.

The best contemporary analogy for this reality comes from the 1999 film *The Matrix,* starring Keanu Reeves and Laurence Fishburne. You may have seen it. Since the inception of this film, the concept of *the red pill* has found its way into our culture's vocabulary.

In the film, Morpheus (Laurence Fishburne) offers the main character Neo (Keanu Reeves) a choice between two pills: a *red pill* and a *blue pill.*

If Neo accepts the *blue pill,* his life remains the same. He goes on living as normal. But if he accepts the *red pill,* life as Neo has known it will never be the same.

The *red pill* Morpheus offers to Neo represents truth or reality. The world that Neo lives in is not real, but imaginary. He, and everyone he knows, lives in this imaginary world.

The *red pill,* however, provides passage for Neo into an alternative universe and reality. Once he takes the *red pill,* he has to fight against everything he has known or perceived in the past as the accepted state of things in order to lay hold of this new and greater reality. Knowing the truth (experiencing that alternative reality) set Neo free from living in an imaginary world.

This truth, or reality, that Neo sought is what Jesus came to present himself as: *I am the truth,* or, *I am what is real.*

There is much more to be learned about Jesus in our walk-through of the Book of John. But from this brief explanation comes the title: JESUS: THE ULTIMATE REALITY. You will find me referring to *the red pill* from time to time throughout the course of this book, and this should be sufficient to explain why.

BOB EMERY

FOREWORD

My greatest challenge in writing this book has not been accumulating the information that's in it. It has always been how to best communicate this information to you.

In the best of worlds, I would choose to relay the contents of this book over a cup of coffee in a cozy, quiet corner of a coffee shop somewhere. During that time, we could freely share our thoughts back and forth with one another, but also laugh, have fun, joke, and ask questions.

*So, with that in mind, after considering other alternatives, what you hold in your hands (or are reading from your computer or smart phone) is the best that I could come up with: a series of short **coffee conversations** that you can read at your leisure to help deepen your understanding of who Jesus is as revealed in probably the most frequently read book in the New Testament, the Book of John.*

So pretend with me, for a moment, that we met in an airport. We spoke only briefly, but what was born out of that conversation was an email I sent to you that went something like this:

> *To my newest friend!*
>
> *I think it was a divine appointment that we met in the coffee line at the airport the other day! It was great to enjoy a cup of coffee together before heading out in different directions on our flights. Our time together was much too short!*
>
> *But in the brief time we did have to talk, I was really taken in by the story you shared with me. Hearing about your newfound love for Jesus and how you gave your life to him was so wonderful! Your life will never be the same!*
>
> *You mentioned to me that you started reading the New Testament and had begun with the Book of John. That's a great place to start. Someone advised you well. Before we parted, you also asked me if there was any good book I could suggest that you read, outside the Bible, that would help you to know Jesus better. I was honored that, after such a brief acquaintance, you would ask.*
>
> *I thought about your question on the plane ride home. There are a lot of good books out there. Funny, but if the truth be told, this is a question that I have thought about off and on for the better part of 50 years, since I first became a Christian. What one book would I*

recommend to a new Christian? I have yet to find a satisfactory answer to that question! No one book comes to mind.

But, I did have this thought that I'll run by you.

I have spent some time in the Book of John over the years. In fact, it is one of my favorite books. What if I were to supplement your reading by sharing some of the things I have learned from John's writing? That would include explanations for some of the new "Christian" vocabulary you will encounter, along with background information that will help you in your understanding of the book.

You can think of this as just an extension of our coffee time together—a morning cup of coffee along with something new to read to get your day started off on the right foot.

How does that sound to you?

Look forward to hearing back from you!

B O B

P.S. And oh, by the way, please greet your two friends who were with you. Though they have not come to know Jesus for themselves yet, they seem like really nice people. Please feel free to share these coffee conversations with them also. Who knows? Maybe within these pages they might even find something helpful in leading them to the truth as well.

TO ALL READERS OF THIS BOOK:

I wish that I could print your individual name at the beginning of each daily coffee conversation. Unfortunately, technology has not come up with a way to do that yet. But what I would like to ask—and I think this will help you get the most out of this book—is that you treat each daily session as a devotional, or as some communication with a personal friend that is writing to you heart to heart. Take it very personally, as if written to you alone. When you've finished each daily reading, take time to reflect and ponder it. And if you feel so led, talk to the Lord about it and ask him to make the things that you have read real for you.

I wish that I could meet with you in person!

May the Lord bless you abundantly.

And may each day be a new opportunity for you to "take the red pill" once again and enter into the reality of knowing Jesus in a fresh, new, and living way.

BOB EMERY

PART ONE | COFFEE CONVERSATIONS

SETTING THE TABLE

WHO WAS JOHN?

I am so looking forward to getting into the Book of John with you. I can't wait!

But before I do, I think it would be helpful to lay some groundwork so that when we get there, you can hit the ground running.

Imagine, with me, building a house. My wife and I try to walk at least three times a week. Our route takes us by a lot where a young man has begun the project of building a house by himself. It is quite an undertaking because he's never done anything like that before.

So far, he has acquired some equipment—a truck, a bulldozer, and a machine that will make bricks out of the soil he'll be moving around to clear the foundation. He started by bulldozing trees and brush to build a road going into the property. Next he brought in a bunch of river rocks and started working on a retaining wall (because it is a steep property). Gradually he'll be bringing other things to the building site like cement, steel reinforcing rods (rebar), wood, shingles, nails, screws, roofing materials, etc. He'll have to bring all these things to the site before he actually starts working on the house itself.

This is what I would like to do in advance of actually coming to the Book of John and using it to build a spiritual foundation in your life. There are some things we need to put in place first, before we actually start to build.

First, I want to introduce you to John, the author. He lived with Jesus for three-and-a-half years. John heard Jesus teach, watched him perform miracles, saw him bless people beyond measure, and also witnessed the way he confronted his adversaries. He laughed with Jesus, cried with Jesus, prayed with Jesus, sang with Jesus, and was brought into the company of other companions who followed Jesus with him.

John and those other early followers found a purpose for their lives that they never had before. Basically, they were all nobodies until Jesus found them, insignificant and unsung men who would be lost to the pages of human history were it not for meeting Jesus. They were witnesses of his ministry from the beginning. Jesus gave them vision and hope. He talked with them about a kingdom. They even grew to think that they were going to be big shots in that kingdom. But then John and the others had another experience in which everything was ripped away. They experienced the cross.

This was the most monumental, horrifying, bone-crushing, and humbling experience John would ever have in his life—to watch Jesus, the one in whom he had put all his hopes, be hung on a tree and crucified.

He and the other men and women whom Jesus had gathered to himself—about 120 people in all—were devastated. They also became afraid because they thought that the same people who crucified Jesus would come after them as well. But then, praise God, John and the others had another experience. They experienced a resurrection! Jesus came back from the dead, met with them again, spent forty days with them in his raised-from-the-dead state, ate with them again, and revealed things that they had not been ready to hear or understand when they only knew him physically. He restored their hope, and then commissioned them and sent them out to change the world!

At our next coffee, I'll introduce you to John a little further, including the experiences and understandings he had of God and God's purpose that qualified him to write his book. I'll also introduce some of the major themes you will encounter as you go through the Book of John. Knowing what to look for before we start will be a great help in grasping the wonderful message it contains!

Looking forward to the journey!

WHO WAS JOHN?
PART TWO

Glad to be with you again today! I'll pick up where I left off yesterday.

The Book of John is named after its author, a disciple and apostle of Jesus named John. A disciple is like an apprentice, a special student of a teacher whose goal is to one day become like his teacher. Apostle means "one who is sent."

Digging down a bit deeper on that word "apostle" brings us to an even greater understanding of what it means to be sent. The Greek word for apostle is actually a military term. An apostle is a person sent out to bring the culture from the place he came from to the place he was going, under the authority of the king. This was happening all over the Roman Empire at the time of Jesus. Soldiers were being dispatched from Rome to different cities throughout the Empire to set up miniature Roman colonies in basically "pagan" cities.

New Testament authors hijacked this term and incorporated it into the vocabulary of their writings. John was one of those apostles sent out to bring the "culture" of the kingdom of heaven, which he had learned from Jesus, to the ends of the earth. Jesus is also referred to in the New Testament as the "Chief Apostle."

Before Jesus called John to be one of his disciples, John was a fisherman. He and his brother, James, along with their business partners, Peter and Andrew—all names you will encounter in the first chapter of John— became part of Jesus' inner circle. John grew up around the Sea of Galilee, close to where Jesus grew up (Nazareth), in the north of Israel. He was the son of Zebedee and Salome. Salome was the sister of Mary, Jesus' mother. This made John one of Jesus' first cousins. The family must have been well-off because during Jesus' three-and-a-half year public ministry, Salome, along with other women, traveled with and helped support Jesus and his team of apostles.

Four different biographies were written about the life and teachings of Jesus. Each one has a slightly different emphasis or perspective. But together, they provide a harmonious unit. These books are also known as the four Gospels (gospel meaning "good news"). All of the authors were either disciples of Jesus or his contemporaries. John's Gospel was probably the last of the four books written.

Some scholars suggest that John's Gospel was written sometime prior to the destruction of Jerusalem and the Temple in the Roman-Jewish war ending in 70 A.D. Others think that it was written later than that— sometime in the 90s. Casting a shadow on this later date view is a verse from John chapter 5 stating that the Temple, colonnades, and the Pool of Bethesda were still in place. John made no mention of this historic and catastrophic event, so it likely hadn't happened yet.

By the end of the war, the Temple was completely destroyed. Not one stone was left standing upon another. This was also something Jesus predicted would happen some forty years earlier, which you can read about in Matthew's Gospel (Matthew 24:2).

If we assume an earlier date then, sometime between 60 and 65 A.D., that would mean that John spent at least thirty-five years with Jesus before writing this book. He had known him both in the flesh (for three-and-a-half years during Jesus' public ministry) and for another thirty-plus years in Spirit, as the resurrected Christ who had come to live inside of him. Putting this in perspective, it is amazing that John was able to reduce all of that time and those experiences he had with Jesus to just about one word for each day spanning that thirty-five-year period.

More tomorrow!

WHO IS GOD?

Back at you again with more on our friend John.

Of the four Gospel accounts, three of them include genealogies. Matthew emphasizes Jesus as the coming king promised to the Jewish people. He traces Jesus' genealogy back to the Old Testament Patriarch Abraham, the Father of the Jewish nation.

Luke highlights Jesus' redemptive work as our Savior. He traces Jesus' genealogy back even farther, to the first man, Adam. Mark's Gospel doesn't contain a genealogy. His emphasis was on Jesus being the Suffering Servant—a prediction about Jesus coming from the Old Testament.

John's Gospel traces Jesus' origin back even further than Abraham or Adam. John begins by introducing us to Jesus as God. John reveals that this Savior, this Servant, this King, *is* the eternal God.

Most people, even unbelievers, would acknowledge that there must be some being, some entity responsible for the existence of the universe. The Bible tells us in Proverbs 14 that only the fool says in his heart there is no God. A computer, with all of its intricate design—a motherboard, processor, power supply, capacity for storage, etc.—did not just evolve or come together without human design. How much more does the creation of the heavens and earth, along with everything on the earth, demand the acknowledgment of a creator, a God?

But who is this God?

The Bible is the best source to answer this question.

The very first sentence in the Bible, Genesis 1:1, begins to introduce us to who God is: "In the beginning God created the heavens and the earth."

The teaching throughout the entire Bible is clear—there is only one God. But right here in the beginning, the Hebrew word translated "God" is *Elohim*. *Elohim* is the plural form of *El* (also meaning "God"), and is used more than 2,500 times in the Old Testament. Not only is the word for God usually used in the plural form, but in places God refers to himself as "Us," as in Genesis 1:26, and other places, where it says, "Then God said, 'Let *Us* make mankind in *Our* image, according to *Our* likeness...'" (NIV *emphasis mine*)

So from the very get-go, we learn that there is one God, the creator of all things, but that there is also a plural dimension to this God. The Bible's full revelation of God teaches us that he exists as Father, Son, and Spirit.

The Bible also tells us that God *is* love. Love describes the essence of his character, his nature.

Theologians will dispute. Philosophers will attempt to answer important questions about the world, the universe, society, and God. The man or woman on the street will give their informed or uninformed opinion. But at the end of the day, the creation will never be able to fully explain the creator. We only know in part. And the older you get and the more you know, as I have found out, the more you will realize how much you don't know. In many ways, God will always remain a mystery.

But as we begin our study of John's Gospel and add to that what we can learn from the rest of the New Testament, we quickly discover that before there was ever a person, a tree, a mountain, or an atom, Jesus Christ was there. Jesus was in the beginning with God and, what's more, he was God. That is how John's Gospel begins! "In the beginning was the Word (Jesus), and the Word was with God, and the Word was God." How awesome is that!

So much more to say about this, but I will leave you hanging until next time to ponder this thought!

THE PLAN OF GOD:
GOD'S ETERNAL PURPOSE

In our last time together, we considered "Who is God?"

Today we're going to look at the plan of God, or God's eternal purpose.

Through John's personal experience and revelation over the years being with Jesus, John not only came to an understanding of who God was, and who Jesus was, but he also came to an understanding of God's eternal purpose. Why did Jesus come? What was the purpose behind his coming? Reduced to its simplest terms, from eternity past, before time even began, God had a plan. That plan motivated him to create the heavens and the earth. The earth would be the stage upon which God's magnificent drama would unfold.

Before the creation, this God we are talking about, who existed as Father, Son, and Spirit, was all that existed! There was nothing outside of him, for he hadn't created anything yet. He was All.

In the invisible, spiritual realm in which this God inhabited, love flowed. There was communion. There was fellowship. The Father loved the Son and the Son loved the Father.

Somewhere along the way, sometime way back there in eternity, before time, God (the Father) had an idea—a thought, a revelation, whatever you want to call it—and it was this: The Father loved the Son so much that he wanted to give him the greatest, most glorious gift ever conceived. That gift was a someone. That someone would be a new being that had never existed before, that would be different than his Son, yet still like him. The best way we can understand this is that God wanted to bring into existence someone that would be like a bride for his Son. She would be someone that he could love with a divine love, someone who would come to know how wonderful he is, and who would love him in return. She would be his life-long companion to walk the halls of eternity forever with him.

This was God's plan—his eternal purpose. And this is what motivated him to create!

God wanted to extend the divine family. He wanted to multiply and expand the relationship, the oneness, the love, the mutual adoration, the fellowship, and the *divine life and nature* that he had shared with his Son, for all eternity, with his creation!

I'll explain more tomorrow. I just wanted to get your attention!

Jesus, the Bridegroom-Lover

That was some pretty heavy stuff I laid on you last time.

But we're just getting started. This is so good! I hope you are as ready to learn more as I am to share more!

It was with this eternal plan in mind—for Jesus to have a bride who he could love, and who would love him in return—that that God began to create.

I'll tell you another little secret. Not only did the invisible God undertake the creation of a physical universe that would be the stage upon which he would implement this plan, but God himself wanted to become visible!

Hold that thought. We'll be coming back to it sometime soon. First, I'd like to take you somewhere else.

I'd like to bring you with me to view the Bible from 40,000 feet up: the big picture view. If you were to read your Bible from cover to cover, and if you were to receive revelation from God, you would arrive at a simple conclusion. The Bible is a love story. It has a bridal theme stretching from Genesis to Revelation. It is a story about Jesus' love for his people: his bride.

In the first book of the Bible, Genesis, chapters one and two, we see hints of God's plan. God created Adam in the Garden of Eden. He gave him a task, to name all the animals. They were created in pairs, male and female. Upon completing this assignment, Adam found that he was the only species on earth that was alone. He had no counterpart that shared a life similar to his.

Then God said that it was not good that man was alone. So he caused a deep sleep to fall upon the man, took one of his ribs, and used that rib to fashion a woman. He then brought the woman to the man, and they were joined in union to become husband and wife. In doing so, they became the mother and father of the whole human race.

This account of the origins of the first man and woman was passed on from mouth to mouth, from generation to generation, until a man named Moses came along and put it into writing. Is this just a story, just a factual account like "God created the heavens and the earth?" Or is it something more? Could it also have been a marker, an illustration or a picture that God placed within the creation to help us understand what the eternal purpose was all about?

I think so. But that is a conclusion that you will have to arrive at on your own as we continue our study of John.

First, allow me to draw these comparisons between Adam and God.

Both experienced "aloneness." Both were the only ones of their species.

Both needed to "die." Adam was put to sleep. Jesus, the Son of God, was crucified, died, and put in the ground for three days.

Both had something taken from within them to help build or fashion their life-partner. A rib was taken from Adam. The Spirit was taken from Jesus.

Both came to life again—Adam to find Eve, his bride, and become one with her, and Jesus to be joined to his bride (the Church) through his life-giving Spirit, and become one with her.

If we have eyes to see it, the first man and the first woman there in Genesis provide the first clear picture of the bridal theme that we will see unfold throughout the whole Bible.

In the last two chapters of the Bible, Revelation 21 and 22 (also written by the Apostle John), we see God's plan completed: a new, recreated heaven and earth, with Jesus' bride (all of God's people) descending out of heaven to become eternally one with him (her Bridegroom) and live on this new earth with him forever.

It is the greatest love story ever told.

This is the story we are introduced to in the Book of John!

From beginning to middle to end and everywhere in between, we see this love story played out with Jesus and his disciples and the other men, women, and children with whom he interacted.

In the beginning of John, Jesus is introduced to us as "the bridegroom" (John 3:29). In the same chapter (3:16) you will find the most quoted Bible verse of all time: "For this is how much God loved the world—he gave his one and only, unique Son as a gift." So now everyone who believes in him will never perish but experience everlasting life" (TPT).

In the middle of John's Gospel, in the final hours before Jesus went to the cross, John wrote of him: "having loved His own who were in the world, He loved them to the end" (John 13:1).

Three times, in the final two chapters, John referred to himself as "the disciple that Jesus loved."

And, notably, the ultimate demonstration of Jesus' love for his bride is that he willingly laid his life down for her on the cross, so that we might live.

The love of God is the major theme of the whole Bible, out of which all other themes flow. We will see this repeatedly in the Book of John.

BEHIND THE SCENES

Last time I made the point that Jesus' quest to have a bride is the main theme of the Bible, from Genesis to Revelation. This bride will be his counterpart—someone like him who shares his life and who will enjoy him and love him for all eternity. And this bride will be taken from the human race.

If I could be so bold, God's purpose is to have a Mrs. God!

Think for a moment about what essential elements are found in almost every great romance story:

- A hero
- A damsel that the hero passionately loves
- An enemy that tries to foil that love, or some conflict that arises that puts the relationship with the damsel in jeopardy
- A rescue, in which the hero overcomes tremendous odds
- The couple lives happily ever after!

So far, we have touched on many of these elements regarding Jesus and his bride. He is the greatest of all heroes; he has a passionate, unconditional love for his bride; he was willing to pay an incredible price to have this life-companion; and we have the assurance that this story ends exceptionally well. The hero gets his gal, and the two of them live happily ever after.

There's one thing, however, missing from these essential love-story elements that we haven't discussed yet: the enemy that stands in the way of the hero and the woman he loves.

The Bible opens in Genesis with the words, "In the beginning God created the heavens and the earth." But the very next words say, "The earth was formless and void (a waste, empty), and darkness was over the surface of the deep, and the Spirit of God was hovering over the surface of the waters."

Another verse from Isaiah says, "For thus says the Lord, who created the heavens, (He is the God who formed the earth and made it, He established it and did not create it a waste place, but formed it to be inhabited)" (Isaiah 45:18, parentheses in original). So you see a conflict here. Which is it? A waste or not a waste? How do we reconcile this?

Here is the subplot. Something happened *after* God originally created the heavens and the earth, but *before* he filled it with the plants, the fish, the birds, the animals, and human beings that you read about in Genesis chapter one. A tragedy took place. The earth became a waste, and darkness completely engulfed it.

Behind the scenes, in the heavenly, unseen realm that God occupies, something else happened. Before the human race was created, God created another form of life that also inhabited the spiritual realm with him. He created the angels. When you study the Bible, you will find a variety of beings mentioned: archangels (those with higher rank than other angels), regular angels, good angels, bad angels, and demons. Demons are actually bad angels.

We are not told the specific details, but piecing together what we learn from the rest of the Bible, at some point one of the three most powerful archangels (those being Lucifer, Michael, and Gabriel) rebelled against God, and a third of the other angels followed him. This was Lucifer, also known by other names such as Satan (the adversary) or the devil (slanderer/accuser). This is where all the problems began.

Some suggest that because he was so beautifully created, Lucifer became proud, and pride led to his fall. There is also evidence that this blinding pride caused him to imagine that he could actually rise above God and usurp God's authority. Finally, elsewhere in the Bible (Psalm 8 and Hebrews chapters 1 and 2 to be specific) we are told that though the angels were created with a life form of their own that was a little higher than humans, they were created to *serve* the human race, not dominate it. In other words, we were the darlings and the focal point of all God's creation. It could also be that because of his pride, when Lucifer learned about the plan of God—that he was actually created to serve us—he became green with jealousy because *he* was not at the center of that plan.

Whatever the exact cause, something disastrous happened to God's beautiful creation. A battle had begun between God and his adversary.

We'll pick up the rest of this story next time.

HOW GOD ACCOMPLISHED HIS PURPOSE

Hope you are enjoying your brew this morning! (Or are you a tea aficionado? Chai, maybe?) I don't know if you prefer dark roast or light, but I'd recommend something strong today. We're going to be wading into deep waters.

We left off last time in the second verse in Genesis where something tragic had happened to the earth God created. Next we read that God spoke again and said, "Let there be light." From there onward, we read the story of creation (or more accurately, the story of re-creation): how God created the light, how he gathered the waters together in their place, and how, on the third day, out of the water dry land appeared. Then life was introduced, beginning with plant life, then fish, then birds, then land animals, and, finally, the pinnacle of his creation: the man and the woman.

God placed this man and woman in a garden. He had a purpose for them. They were to bear the image of God and rule over the earth that he had created. He also put two specific trees in the Garden, among all the others. One was called the tree of life, and the other, the tree of the knowledge of good and evil.

He placed only one restriction on the man and the woman (Adam and Eve): not to eat of that second tree because, if they did, they would surely die.

It does not take long for the second great tragedy to occur in Genesis, and this is the one that has had the greatest impact on us up to this very minute!

Satan appeared to Adam and Eve in the form of a serpent, a snake. He cunningly persuaded them to listen to him by telling them a lie. If they ate of that second tree, they would not die, but they would become like God, and know good and evil.

Sadly, they took the bait. Because they rebelled and sinned against God (as Satan did), this plunged the whole human race into a fallen state, and our authority to rule the earth was usurped. We came under the dominion of this fallen angel. As a result, God removed Adam and Eve from the Garden and blocked the way for them to return.

God had intended for them to eat from the tree of life, but they lost their opportunity.

And think about it. If God had left them in the Garden and allowed them to eat of the tree of life and live forever, what a disaster that would have been! They would have lived forever in a fallen state, eternally shackled to a marred existence!

This delayed the fulfillment of God's purpose, but it could never deny it. In order to remedy this situation and provide a way for the human race to access the tree of life once again, Jesus needed to come to earth and become our Savior.

For Jesus to accomplish this purpose required a two-step process. First, he needed to die on the cross, bearing the consequences of sin for us, which was death and separation from God. By believing in him and his substitutionary death (him instead of us), we can be forgiven of our sins and restored into relationship with God once more, as was always intended.

It is as if we are empty bottles created for an extraordinary purpose—to contain pure, thirst-quenching water from a fresh mountain spring. But before realizing that purpose, those bottles dropped to the ground and rolled in the mud. They became filthy. Our Lord's first job, then, was to clean the bottles. This he did through his death on the cross.

Having cancelled out our sin-debt, making us righteous, holy, and clean in his sight, he could then move on to step two: restoring the original purpose he had for us as those bottles. That was to fill us with his life, by his Spirit. "For this is how much God loved the world—he gave his one and only, unique Son *as a gift*. So now everyone who believes in him will never perish but experience everlasting life" (John 3:16 TPT).

This offer to "everyone" left no one out. It is for every man, woman, and child who chooses to receive the free gift of forgiveness and eternal life. From the very beginning, our salvation and redemption was never about what we could do for God to earn or merit that salvation. It has always been the result of God's extravagant generosity to give beyond anything we deserve (referred to in the Bible as "God's grace").

You will see this in the illustrations of Jesus' interactions with people throughout the Book of John. As you read, aided by the illumination of the Holy Spirit, you will also see there is at least one main lesson—and more often than not, many lessons—to be learned in each illustration, person, and sign John selected to write about. John not only used personal encounters Jesus had with different people to capture some of Jesus' teaching; these stories also reveal something about Jesus' nature, something that clearly made a deep impression on John and the other apostles. In each encounter, Jesus demonstrated that he was "full of grace and truth" (John 1:14). To experience and to behold the grace of God—to come to a real understanding of the truth of God—is life changing. It is transforming. These were the experiences that changed the disciples, made them fall in love with Jesus, want to be more like him, and want to share the message of his life.

At the end of John's Gospel (chapter 20, verses 30-31), John explained his purpose for writing it: "...many other signs Jesus also performed in the presence of the disciples, which are not written in this book; but these have been written so that you may believe that Jesus is the Christ [the Messiah, the Sent One], the Son of God; and that believing, you may have *life* in His name" (*emphasis mine*). This message is reinforced by other New Testament authors like the Apostle Paul when he wrote to his disciple and co-worker Timothy saying, "Take hold of the eternal life to which you were called" (1 Timothy 6:12), or the Apostle Peter, who encouraged his readers that they had become "partakers of the divine nature" (2 Peter 1:4).

Having completed this background material that will give us a good foundation to study the Book of John—an introduction to the author, an introduction to God and God's eternal purpose, the motif of God as our bridegroom and lover, what was happening behind the scenes, and how God accomplished his purpose—next I want to highlight some of the major themes you will encounter in John's Gospel. This is where it really starts getting good!

Major Themes in the Book of John

THE SPEAKING GOD WANTS TO COMMUNICATE WITH YOU

Good to be with you again!

So far we've covered a lot of background information about the nature of God and God's purpose. We're almost ready to dive into the Book of John itself (I promise!), but I think you'll get more out of the book once you are aware of some of the major themes to be on the lookout for.

Right out of the gate, John refers to Jesus as "the Word." This is our first theme: God is a speaking God.

In order for us to know the heart of a person—what they are like, what they are thinking, what they are feeling—they need to express their desires, thoughts, and feelings through words. Through their words, the nature of a person is revealed. That's why Jesus is referred to as the Word of God. The invisible God wanted to reveal and express himself to mankind, and the person through whom he does that is his Son, Jesus Christ.

The Bible begins in Genesis with God creating the world from nothing by speaking it into existence. Throughout the Old Testament he spoke to the prophets and to his people:

- He spoke to Adam in the Garden.
- In Genesis 6:13 he spoke to Noah, commanding him to build a boat.
- In Genesis 15:1 he spoke to Abraham saying, "Do not fear. I am a shield to you. Your reward shall be very great."
- In Exodus 33:11: "Thus the Lord used to speak to Moses face to face, just as a man speaks to his friend."
- In I Samuel 3:4 he spoke to Samuel.
- In II Samuel 7:4, "The word of the Lord also came to Nathan."
- In I Chronicles 22:7-8, "The word of the Lord came to David saying, "You shall not build a house..."
- In I Kings 6:11 he spoke to Solomon.
- In 2 Samuel 24:11 he spoke to Gad.
- In I Kings 12:22 he spoke to Shemaiah, the man of God.
- In II Kings 3:12 he spoke to Elisha.
- In II Kings 20:4 he spoke to Isaiah.
- In Ezekiel 1:3 he spoke to Ezekiel.
- In Jeremiah 1:4 he spoke to Jeremiah.
- In Joel 1:1 he spoke to Joel.
- In Hosea 1:1 he spoke to Hosea.
- In Jonah 1:1 he spoke to Jonah.
- In Micah 1:1 he spoke to Micah.
- In Zephaniah 1:1 he spoke to Zephaniah.
- In Haggai 1:1 he spoke to Haggai.
- In Zechariah 1:1 the word of the Lord came to Zechariah.
- In Malachi 1:1 he spoke to Malachi.

Finally, more than 2,000 years ago, God himself stepped into his creation, put on human flesh, and this Word took up residence inside the human body of Jesus. Now the living God would not only reveal himself to his creation through his words, but by becoming visible, he would show us who he was by his actions.

The words Jesus speaks are life-giving words. Here are some examples of things he said, according to the Book of John:

> Truly, truly, I say to you, he who hears My word and
> believes Him who sent Me has eternal life.
> JOHN 5:24

> I assure you: An hour is coming, and is now here, when
> the dead will hear the voice of the Son of God, and those
> who hear will live . . . all who are in the graves will hear
> His voice and come out—those who have done good
> things, to the resurrection of life, but those who have
> done wicked things, to the resurrection of judgment.
> JOHN 5:25,28&29 HCSB

> It is the Spirit who gives life; the flesh profits nothing; the
> words that I have spoken to you are spirit and are life.
> JOHN 6:63

> And finally, Peter spoke to Jesus one day and said, "Lord,
> to whom shall we go? You have the words of eternal life."
> JOHN 6:68

That's really all that I wanted to share with you today. John wanted you to understand, right from the first, that God is a speaking God. Expect, in this new relationship you now have with him, that he wants to talk with you. As you read through the Book of John you will see that God communicates with people through Jesus in both his words and his actions. Look for this theme as you read.

It will take some time to learn to hear and discern God's voice because you're just a beginner at this. We all are. But I promise, as you begin to desire God and seek him, he will begin to speak to you and you will begin to recognize his voice.

Take that to the bank. That's a promise!

JESUS CAME TO BE YOUR LIFE

This is probably one of the most important, if not *the* most important, theme you'll find in the Book of John: life.

John begins his gospel with, "In the beginning was the Word, and the Word was with God, and the Word was God." He continues to say that, "Life was in Him, and that life was the light of men", and concludes this thought by explaining that this "Word became flesh and took up residence among us. We observed His glory, the glory as the One and Only Son from the Father, full of grace and truth" (v.1, 4, and 14 HCSB).

The highest life in the universe, the creator God, came to this earth in the person of Jesus and manifest his life among us. The nature of that life was not like human life: it was eternal, uncreated, incorruptible, indestructible, and divine. The Greek word to describe this life of God in the New Testament is the word *zoe*, the life form that is attributed to God alone.

Jesus said things like:

> For just as the Father has life in Himself, even so He gave
> the Son to have life in Himself.
> JOHN 5:26

35

> For just as the Father raises the dead and gives them life,
> even so the Son also gives life to whom He wishes.
>
> JOHN 5:21

And he stated his purpose and mission for coming: "I have come that you might have *life* [Greek word: *zoe*] and that you might have it in abundance" (John 10:10, *emphasis mine*).

That word "life" is used more in the Gospel of John (and in John's other writings) than in any of the other gospels or New Testament letters.

In John we see Jesus as:

» The Bread of Life

» The Water of Life

» The Light of Life

» The Resurrection and the Life

» The Way, the Truth, and the Life

» The Giver of Life

Some people quote Jesus' words, "I have come to give life and to give it in abundance," and assume that means Jesus came to give you a bunch of good stuff. Not so at all! That doesn't mean that he won't bless you by giving you good things, but he has a different meaning in mind.

First, I'll tell you what he was *not* saying, and then I'll tell you what he meant. He was not promising that he would make everyone's life cushy. The "abundant life" that Jesus promised had nothing to do with your circumstances—great home, great car, great bank account, great job, great health, great friends, a great family, and the like. What Jesus WAS promising, though, was even better! Paraphrased, it goes like this: "I have come to give you life—MY life, *zoe* life, the eternal, uncreated, incorruptible, indestructible life that I share with my Father and have lived by for all eternity. THIS is the life that I have come to give you! And I want to give it to you in abundance!"

When you read the Book of John, keep an eye out for this word "life." Follow this life that is in God. It starts in God, but it ends up in you!

If any of us were to *really* grasp what Jesus is saying here we'd leap right out of our skins. You might even want to jump out of your chair right now, rush up to the barista, grab him or her by their ears, give them a big, sloppy kiss, and then shout, "Hallelujah!"

(That might be overdoing it a little, but at the very least, I should think that you would get excited!)

LIFE STANDS IN OPPOSITION TO MAN-MADE RELIGION

As you read about the ministry of Jesus Christ, you will see that the people welcomed him. His miracles, his teachings, his wisdom, and his good works amazed them. They had hopes that he would be the Messiah.

(Quick side note: "Messiah" is a word you will encounter a number of times in the Book of John and elsewhere in the New Testament. Messiah was a Hebrew term that means "Anointed One" or "Chosen One." The Greek word equivalent to the Hebrew word Messiah is *Christos,* or in English, *Christ.* "Christ" was not Jesus' last name, but a title given to him by his followers: "Jesus, the Messiah." In Old Testament times, a priest would pour a blend of oil and sweet smelling perfumes on the head of a new king or other special official to "anoint" him, inaugurating his reign. Calling Jesus "Christ" was therefore like calling him God's chosen king.)

But gradually the religious leaders of the day began to plant doubts in the people's minds about Jesus' credibility. These leaders clung to their traditions and authority structure because their security was based on their place in the religious system. Anything new or disruptive, they viewed with suspicion. This ultimately led them to reject Jesus and crucify him.

Jesus challenged these leaders. He challenged their traditions, their corruption, their legalism, and the misguided ways in which they interpreted the Scriptures. I think it's fair to point out that this same practice happens today within many quarters of the Christian church. This misinterpretation can turn people off to what Jesus and Christianity are really about.

Who were these religious leaders? Let's put jerseys on them so we can identify them. They were:

- The Pharisees: experts in the Jewish law, who believed in strict adherence to the law and Jewish traditions as the pathway to holiness.

- The Sadducees: a priestly class that rejected teachings on the resurrection of the dead and the afterlife. They believed that once we die, that's it. They also didn't believe that angels or demons existed.

- The scribes: ancient Jewish record-keepers; they were designated to make hand-written copies of the Scriptures, and also acted as professional theologians and jurists.

- The priests: those who officiated at the Temple.

The religious leaders intimidated the common people against believing that Jesus was the Messiah. If individuals were to believe—and proclaim so publically—the leaders would throw them out of the Temple (John 9:22), making them outcasts. Confessing to be a follower of Jesus ostracized individuals from their friends, family, and the rest of their community that participated in the Temple services. There was tremendous pressure to stick to the status quo.

But Jesus did not hold back from confronting the fabricated, man-made religion of the Jewish leaders, 1) because he still loved them and wanted them to know the truth, and 2) because their religion was taking them in another direction, away from the truth. One day he got into it with that group and said to them,

> The Father who sent Me, He has testified of Me. You have
> neither heard His voice at any time nor seen His form.
> You do not have His word abiding in you for you do not
> believe Him whom He sent. You search the Scriptures
> because you think that in them you have eternal life; it
> is these that testify about Me; and you are unwilling to
> come to Me so that you may have life.
> JOHN 5:37-40

On another day, Jesus broke the Jewish Sabbath (their day of rest) by healing an invalid at the Pool of Bethesda. These religious Jews were so hard-core and clung so tightly to the letter of the laws handed down to them by Moses that they often missed the spirit of the law. Jesus had to shake that up, which constantly put him at odds with them. This added to Jesus' unpopularity, and the religious leaders ultimately decided to find a way to kill him.

Jesus told the Jews, "If I bear witness of Myself, My witness is not true" (John 5:31).

In other words, if Jesus just made claims about himself, that was not enough. Other witnesses needed to corroborate that what he was saying about himself was true. So he gave the people other witnesses and a number of chances to get it right, but at each opportunity many of them rejected him and their hearts grew harder.

- First, there was the witness of John the Baptizer. John was sent to them as a forerunner, announcing the coming of the Messiah. In chapter 40 of the Book of Isaiah, Isaiah prophesied that one would come who would prepare the way of the Lord and announce his coming, saying to Jerusalem and the cities of Judah, "Behold your God!" John did just that. He testified that he saw the Spirit of God descend upon Jesus and stay with him. He (as well as others) heard God's audible voice from heaven testify that Jesus was God's Son, in whom he was well pleased. But most Jews ultimately rejected John's testimony.

- There was the witness of his miracles: healing the sick, giving sight to the blind, raising the dead, feeding 5,000 people with only a few fish and pieces of bread, walking on water, etc.

- There was the witness of his teaching, his wisdom, his mercy, and his compassion.

- And there was the witness of the Scriptures that testified about him.

Despite all of this evidence and opportunity to believe, large numbers of the Jews still rejected him.

Finally, Pontius Pilate, the Roman governor of Judea who presided at Jesus' trial, examined the charges the Jews made against him, and ultimately gave the order for his crucifixion:

> He said, "Behold, I am bringing Him out to you so that
> you may know that I find no guilt in Him..." So when

the chief priests and the officers saw Him, they cried out saying, "Crucify, crucify!" Pilate said to them, "Take Him yourselves and crucify Him, for I find no guilt in Him."

JOHN 19:4, 6

This was the ultimate opposition and rejection—to put him to death.

Even beyond this, after they crucified him, more evidence of Jesus' authority was given. The stone in front of his tomb was rolled away and his body was gone, testifying that he had risen from the dead. Tens of thousands of people in Jerusalem and beyond witnessed to the fact that he was alive. Still many did not believe.

But God still had mercy. In the interim between the resurrection and the destruction of the Temple in 70 A.D., a number priests changed their minds and became followers of Jesus. The Book of Acts records, "The word of God kept on spreading; and the number of disciples continued to increase greatly in Jerusalem, and a great many of the priests were becoming obedient to the faith" (Acts 6:7). But the majority did not. In fact, it was the Jews who took a prominent role in the persecution of Christians in Judea and throughout the Roman Empire. Only a remnant ended up believing and became part of the first-century church.

This is a lesson you also will learn as you go through the Book of John and mature in the Christian life: Religion, no matter what form it takes, blinds people's eyes to Jesus. Man-made religion always opposes Jesus, and Jesus, the living God, always opposes religion.

Jesus is Light and the Holy Spirit

I'm anxious to get into the actual Book of John with you. To speed things along, I thought I'd identify two themes today. The first one has to do with Light, and the second, with the Holy Spirit.

Let's go back again to those potent, power-packed verses at the beginning of John. John 1:4-5 says, "Life was in Him, and that life was the light of men. That light shines in the darkness, yet the darkness did not overcome it" (HCSB).

John 1:9 says, "The true [real] light, who gives light to everyone, was coming into the world" (HCSB).

John 8:12 says, "Then Jesus again spoke to them, saying, 'I am the Light of the world; he who follows Me will not walk in the darkness, but will have the Light of life.'"

John 12:46 says, "I have come as Light into the world, so that everyone who believes in Me will not remain in darkness."

Jesus is the true light, or the *real* light. I'll get into that more with you tomorrow. For now, just remember to keep an eye out for references to light as you read through the Book of John.

Another theme in John is the Holy Spirit.

Both the Hebrew and the Greek word for "spirit" can also mean wind, breath, or air. Like God's Spirit, these things cannot be seen, but they are real and vital for life.

Jesus compared himself to wind: "The wind blows where it wishes and you hear the sound of it, but do not know where it comes from and where it is going; so is everyone who is born of the Spirit" (John 3:8).

In John chapter 1 (v. 33) Jesus is introduced to us as the one who "baptizes with the Holy Spirit." I'll be talking about that more once we get into the Book of John.

Jesus told his disciples that they would be receiving the Holy Spirit: "But this He spoke of the Spirit, whom those who believed in Him were to receive; for the Spirit was not yet *given*, because Jesus was not yet glorified" (John 7:39).

Jesus told his disciples that the Spirit they were to receive would be with them forever. Then he got a little mystical on them. "I will ask the Father, and He will give you another Helper, that He may be with you forever. That is the Spirit of truth, whom the world cannot receive, because it does not see Him or know Him. But you know Him because He abides with you and will be in you. I will not leave you as orphans; I will come to you" (John 14:16-18).

Here's my paraphrased version of these verses: "I'm going to be physically leaving you. But I'll ask my Father and he's going to send someone to help you—the Spirit of truth. The world won't get it. But you will. This helper, this Spirit, is living *with* you right now and will be *in* you. I won't abandon you; *I* will come back to you, but in a different form, as the Spirit."

Jesus also told his disciples that the Holy Spirit would teach them all things, guide them into all truth, speak to them, remind them of the all that he said to them, and tell them things to come (John 14:26 and 16:13). Finally, after his resurrection, while in an upper room with the disciples, Jesus breathed on them and said, "Receive the Holy Spirit" (John 20:22).

God was Spirit, Christ was Spirit, then Jesus stepped out of the invisible realm and came to earth to live among us. The Spirit was in Christ, then the Spirit ended up in the disciples, and now the Spirit is in you!

This is a pretty cool message, isn't it?

That is why the gospel means, "Good News!"

JESUS IS FULL OF
GRACE & TRUTH (REALITY)

I have two more themes for you today that show up in the Book of John. And they are big ones. One concerns something Jesus does, the other, who he is.

There's a verse from the first chapter of John that I've mentioned to you already, but I want to circle back to it. It is John 1:14: "The Word became flesh and took up residence among us. We observed His glory, the glory as the One and Only Son from the Father, full of grace and truth" (HCSB).

Let's break this verse down a little.

Before we get to "grace and truth" let's first talk about "glory." What is "glory?" One dictionary definition is "magnificence or great beauty." That's OK. But let me suggest another definition: Glory is God expressed. When John said that they saw his glory, he was saying that they saw God's perfect, divine attributes—including his magnificence, beauty, power, kindness, and love—all on display and being expressed in the person of Jesus.

Earlier I defined "grace" for you as God's extravagant generosity to give beyond anything we deserve. Others define grace as the "outpouring of God's unmerited favor and love toward us," which it is. Both are true.

A dear friend of mine came up with more of an "out of the box" definition that I had never heard before. He said that grace is "God's unstoppable, relentless, effortless nature to give." I like that!

Jesus was constantly demonstrating his love by the grace he showed toward helpless, sinful, and needy people through the signs he performed and his interactions with them.

The second theme revolves around this word "truth." In the Introduction, I mentioned that the Greek word that translates into the English word "truth" is *altetheia*, which carries with it the meaning of reality, that which is real.

Before the heavens and the earth existed, God was all there was. He *was* reality. That reality was spiritual in nature. And it was invisible.

Then God created the heavens and the earth and filled them with shadows, pictures, and types mirroring heavenly realities. He left his fingerprints—identifying markers—everywhere. He did this to provide you with things that you could see, feel, and touch that would help you understand what the invisible God is like.

Here are some examples: God created water, which is necessary for our survival. Yet Jesus said that he would give us *living* water—water that is *alive*—and that he was that water. He created the grains, by which we make physical bread to eat. Yet Jesus taught that he was the *living* bread that came down out of heaven to give life to the world. He created luminaries in the heavens. Yet said that he was the Light of the world.

He created lambs that were for centuries offered as sacrifices on account of sins, and he did this to prepare us to understand that he was the *real* Lamb of God who came as the ultimate sacrifice to take away the sin of the world.

If you look for it, you'll see this so clearly in the Book of John.

To refer back to the analogy of the Matrix once more, this world we live in *is* the Matrix. It is filled with shadows. Shadows are not real—they are only images. The object that casts the shadow is that which has substance and is real. Once you take the big red pill, your eyes will be opened to an unseen reality behind all that your eyes can see. That reality *is* Jesus Christ!

JESUS, THE TRUE (REAL) VINE

Another theme in the Book of John is the theme of abiding, or resting in Jesus. Some background on this theme can also be found in the Genesis story of creation (or, re-creation).

God worked for six days creating everything. On the sixth day, he created the man and the woman. This was the finale of his creation. Then it says that God rested on the seventh day from all his work.

God rested, not because he was all tired, sweaty, and worn out—God never gets tired. He rested because his work of creation was finished.

Once God created the man and the woman and placed them in a beautiful Garden in Eden (Eden means "paradise"), he gave them instructions. Genesis says, "God blessed them [made them very happy!]; and God said to them, "Be fruitful and multiply, and fill the earth, and subdue it; and rule over the fish of the sea and over the birds of the sky and over every living thing that moves on the earth." (Every living thing, by the way, included the creeping things and the serpent, which they failed to subdue.)

Adam and Eve probably went to bed that night saying to themselves,

"Oh boy, this is great! Can't wait to get started in the morning with this multiplying thing and ruling and subduing this beautiful place that God has created for us!"

But they awoke to a surprise! Their *first* day would be the seventh day—God's day of rest. Before they did one ounce of work, God wanted them to just rest with him and enjoy being with God. The following day they could begin working, tilling the garden, cultivating fruit, and looking for enemies to conquer and subdue.

With this in mind, let's return to the Book of John (chapter 15) and look at what Jesus meant when he said, "I am the real vine."

Once again, consider our metaphor from *The Matrix*. The red pill represents passage into an alternative reality, a reality overlapping but distinct from the world that you see. As part of his creation, God created trees and vines. Those trees and vines bear fruit—apples, oranges, tangerines, grapes, etc. Physical trees and plants bear physical fruit. But these trees and fruits are only a picture—a mirror of some heavenly reality that God wants us to understand.

In his letter to the Christians living in the Galatia region, which is now part of southern Turkey, the Apostle Paul described the "fruit" of the Spirit as "love, joy, peace, patience, kindness, goodness, gentleness, faithfulness, and self-control" (Galatians 5:22-23).

Jesus told his early disciples, "I am the true [real] vine, and My Father is the vinedresser" (John 15:1). A few verses later (v. 4) he said, "I am the vine, you are the branches; he who abides in Me and I in him bears much fruit, for apart from Me you can do nothing" (John 15:5).

Do you get it?

Jesus used a vine to describe himself.

What Jesus was saying was, if you abide in me (once I come into you by means of the Spirit), because I abide in you, the rich strength and nutrients of *my* life will naturally flow through you, which will cause you to effortlessly bear spiritual fruit and become like me. Bearing fruit does not require work and self-effort, it requires abiding in Jesus and resting in him.

The word "abide" means to remain. Just remain in Jesus. That is the secret to the Christian life. Receive Jesus! Abide in Jesus! Rest in Jesus!

Abiding in Christ does not mean that we will experience perpetual spiritual ecstasy and always be living on some emotional high. Much of the time our souls will just be at rest as we experience his peace and sense his life within us, even while passing through difficult times. But if we stray from the Lord and/or sin, we will become aware that our hearts have turned away and that we are not abiding in him.

Incidentally, Jesus also used the vine as an illustration for another reason. Mahogany, oak, and cherry are hardwoods. They are useful, beautiful, and can be used for building things. But a vine is useless. You can't build anything with it. The vine itself is so twisted and gnarly that it's not very nice to look at. It is only good for one thing: bearing fruit. We can't produce the kind of fruit that God is looking for on our own. We can only produce fruit as we abide and rest in him. I'll have more to say about the vine later when we get to it in our study.

SUMMARY

All that you have read to this point has been background information to introduce you to the beautiful Book of John.

If I could distill everything that has been written so far and give you one simple takeaway to remember, it would be this:

Like no other book in the Bible, John's Gospel presents Jesus Christ as the infinite God who created all things and then came from the heavenly realm to this earth to present himself as the spiritual reality behind all things vital to sustain life. He presented himself as *real* food, drink, light, air (breath, wind), and rest. His motivation was love. He loved you so much that he wanted you to enter into that spiritual reality with him.

PART 3

The Beautiful Book of John

THE ETERNAL GOD BECAME A MAN

CHAPTER 1

Here we go! We've finally made it to the Book of John!

Open up your Bible to the first page in the Book of John. It's the fourth book in the New Testament on page 1713. (Just kidding! That's in my Bible. I don't know what translation you are using.)

Reading the first few lines in the Book of John, is like seeing a falling star streak across the night sky. It goes by you so fast that you barely have time to see it: Jesus Christ is God, was God, and has existed with God from before all time. He is Life. He is Light. And like a candle in a dark room, darkness cannot overcome him.

These concepts are simple, yet profound. On the surface, they may seem easy to understand, but they're also deep and defy understanding.

God wants to reveal who he is to you. So as you begin this journey through the Book of John, read slowly. Don't treat it as you would an online political story or movie review—quickly, flying over it, and trying to take in everything all at once.

Savor the words. Taste the words. And then at different intervals, when you sense you are receiving a new impression or understanding, respond to the Word himself in your own words by talking with him. This is what God wants—relationship! Use your Bible reading time as a time to build that relationship. Talk to him, and he will talk to you. Keep it simple, and just look for opportunities to enjoy Jesus.

This God, who always was, who is the possessor of the highest most creative life in the universe, and who is full of light, one day stepped out of the unseen realm of eternity and came to earth in the form of a man. John and the other disciples who walked with him and lived with him, saw his glory—his beauty, his magnificence, his splendor—like no one else who had ever lived. He was full of grace and truth.

This same God, this same Jesus, is the One who has now stepped into your life. This might be another good place to stop and pause and, in your own words, say something to him like, " Dear Lord, you are so full of grace. I love you. Thank you for coming for me." Or, "Jesus, you appeared to John and the other disciples and showed them your glory, your grace, and your truth. I want you to show yourself to me in the same way so that I can know and love you more."

Well, I think we need to stop here. This has been a short session together, but that's a lot to think about for one day! Go back to your Bible and take a few minutes to just pause and meditate on these weighty truths. I look forward to being back with you in the morning!

Cheers!

DAY 15

JOHN THE BAPTIST'S MISSION & THE LAMB OF GOD

CHAPTER 1

We're back at it!

Today I'd like to introduce you to a new character. You may have heard him referred to as John the Baptist.

This guy was one of the weirdest dudes in the entire Bible. First of all, he was not a Baptist in the way we most often use that word today. "Baptist" is a Christian denomination (like Catholics, Presbyterians, Lutherans, Methodists, etc.), and they don't come on the scene for another 1600 years! In his day, John was known as John the *baptizer*.

In the Old Testament, the prophet Isaiah predicted some 700 years earlier that just before God's special representative was revealed, another prophet (John) would announce his coming. You can learn more about the baptizer in the other gospel accounts. I'll try to make this introduction brief.

John was six months older than Jesus. He, like Jesus, was also a miracle baby. But his miraculous birth was nowhere as great as Jesus, whose mother, Mary, was a virgin.

At an early age, John's parents sent him out into the wilderness to be raised in an Essene community. The Essenes were a religious bunch that lived out in the desert, away from the cities and crowds. They practiced celibacy and pursued virtuous living. Their goal was to escape from the world and live quiet and simple lives.

John's parents probably sent John there at a very young age because not long after his birth a mad, paranoid king named Herod went on a killing rampage, ordering the murder all the children ages two and below in and around Jerusalem. Herod had learned from some astrologers—who had traveled from the East, following an unusually bright star—that a new king (Jesus) had been born, and Herod feared a challenger to his throne. Most likely, John's parents heard about this berserk king ordering the indiscriminate slaughter of babies, and they believed that hiding John in the desert was the best way to preserve his life.

John was about the farthest thing from a fashion icon or pretentious foodie that you could possibly imagine. (That's why I referred to him as one really weird dude!) He dressed in camel's skin, secured around the waist by a leather belt. His diet consisted of crunchy locust crackers, covered by wild honey. (Imagine a steady diet of grasshoppers!)

God spoke to John at some point when he was in the desert. He told John to preach a message of repentance to the people, telling them that they needed to change their minds, get their hearts right, and shape up, because the promised One was about to come. Multitudes from Jerusalem and other cities began coming out to the desert to listen to John. As a sign that they received his message and were willing to clean up their lives, John would ceremoniously dunk them in water—often, the Jordan River.

But God also told John that one of those that he would dunk in the water would have the Spirit of God descend upon him. This was the One he was to look for.

You can imagine people coming to John for baptism and John sizing them up: "No, its not you." "Nope, surely you're not the one." And if you were there when the pompous Pharisees came out to him, you would have heard him thinking out loud, "No way can it be you! You brood of vipers! Why should I waste my time baptizing you? I know that none of you could be the Messiah!"

It would not be surprising if at times during this assignment John became disappointed and discouraged. After baptizing probably thousands of people and not seeing the extraordinary or miraculous results that God had promised, he could possibly have questioned his calling.

But then one day Jesus came to him and was baptized. John saw the Spirit of God descend on Jesus like a dove and rest upon him. Finally, John's mission was accomplished. God opened his eyes to see that this Jesus was the promised One. John responded by declaring, "Look! There he is—God's Lamb! He will take away the sins of the world!" (TPT).

Jesus came as the spotless, sacrificial Lamb of God, born to die, born to forgive the world of their sins.

God also told John that the One on whom the Spirit would fall would baptize in the Holy Spirit. What does that mean? To baptize something means to put it completely under water, to immerse it. If you "baptized" a piece of white paper into a bucket of red paint, it would come out red.

What that means for you is this: God has big plans for you. You may have started out as one thing, but once God has immersed you in his Spirit, you come out transformed and changed into something else! You become a new creature. I'll have more to say about this as we go along.

Enjoy your coffee!

DAY 16

JESUS, THE SON OF MAN

CHAPTER 1

I hope that you are enjoying your brew this morning!

In the next story we come to in John's Gospel, Jesus began to call individuals to follow him. One of these men, Andrew, told his brother, Peter, "We have found the Messiah." (You will see Peter come up a number of times in John's Gospel. He was prominent among the apostles. His original name was Simon, but one day when God gave him a revelation that Jesus was the Messiah, Jesus gave him a new name—Peter, which meant "a rock").

The day that Jesus began calling people to follow him must have been glorious and emotional for him. Finally, after an eternity of waiting, for the first time, he laid physical eyes on some of the men who would be part of that cosmic, corporate bride that I shared about with you earlier. His eternal purpose was now playing out in time and space. He called them to follow him and they willingly responded. He couldn't have helped but be overjoyed!

At the beginning of the first chapter of John, John introduced Jesus as God. By the end of the first chapter, he referred to him by another title, "the Son of Man." This expression "the Son of Man" appears eighty-one times in the four Gospels: thirty times in Matthew, fourteen times in Mark, twenty-five times in Luke, and twelve times in John.

Technically, the word "man" here is not a specific reference to the male gender. It could be better understood as "son of all mankind" or "son of the human race." Even as far back as the first chapter in Genesis, when God created the man and the woman, the Bible says, "Then God said, 'Let us make mankind in our image, in our likeness, so that they may rule over the fish in the sea and the birds in the sky, over the livestock and all the wild animals and over all the creatures that move along the ground.' So God created mankind in his own image, in the image of God he created them; male and female he created them" (Genesis 1:26-27 NIV). God needed the characteristics of both the man *and* the woman to represent his image; to convey and express characteristics of what he is like. (Ruminate on that for a moment...)

So that's some background on the term "Son of Man." Since many Bible translations use that term, we'll just go with it; it's a phrase you're likely to come across. But, don't forget: it does take two to tango. It takes more than a man to give birth to a son. That requires a woman as well!

Getting back to the script: you may be wondering why Jesus referred to himself more often as the Son of Man, rather than the Son of God. Why would he do that? Way back in Genesis, after the fall of man, God made a promise that from the seed of a woman one would come from the human race who would destroy the devil and his work (Genesis 3:15). This was the first mention of God's intention to send the Messiah into this world, and that this Messiah would appear in human flesh.

Jesus' reference to himself as the Son of Man also alludes to a promise made through the prophet Daniel in the Old Testament (Daniel 7:13-14) that the Messiah would ascend to the Father after being raised from the dead:

> I continued watching in the night visions, and I saw One like a son of man coming with the clouds of heaven. He approached the Ancient of Days and was escorted before Him. He was given authority to rule, and glory, and a kingdom; so that those of every people, nation, and language should serve Him. His dominion is an everlasting dominion that will not pass away, and His kingdom is one that will not be destroyed. HCSB

After Jesus died and was raised from the dead on the third day, he ascended to heaven to be re-united with his Father. There, in invisible realms, he was crowned Lord of all and given a kingdom comprised of people from every nation, tribe, and tongue.

Not only did Jesus ascend, but also somehow, mysteriously, *we* ascended with him. He brought us *with him* into that realm from which he came, and into the presence of his Father to make us part of the divine family.

And that family is big! Like the stars in the sky, they are beyond number and cannot be counted.

In your journey with God you will meet other brothers and sisters from around the world, from different nations, tribes, and tongues that share the same divine life with God as you do. They are now part of *your* new family as well!

What an inheritance you have been given! That's a lot to give thanks for.

GRACE FOR THE UNDESERVING—THE WEDDING AT CANA OF GALILEE

CHAPTER 2

Next we come to chapter 2, and immediately we read about the first miracle Jesus performed. It happened at a wedding in a town called Cana of Galilee.

It was not accidental or insignificant that the first sign and miracle Jesus performed was at a wedding. John was giving us a clue—our first real insight into the mysterious purpose behind Jesus' coming.

Jesus' mother noticed that the hosts had run out of wine. This was about to cause great embarrassment for the bridegroom and his bride, so she turned to Jesus and essentially said, "This is about to get bad. Can you do something about this?"

Jewish culture in those days was very rigid, law-oriented, and unforgiving. Those who made mistakes had to pay the consequences. Grace was a rare commodity.

Not having enough wine at a wedding party could easily have stigmatized the parents, the bridegroom, and the bride of this village indefinitely. It could have made them the brunt of jokes and scorn.

But that day, Jesus treated the situation in a way that none would have expected. Wanting to see honor, and not embarrassment (which they justifiably would have deserved because of poor planning), come to the hosts on that special day, Jesus turned six large jars full of ordinary water into the best wine that anyone had ever tasted. Not only did he rescue the situation, but the wedding guests were also left with the impression that the bridegroom was a man of great honor by saving the best wine for last. Only the servants and the disciples seemed to really know who was responsible for this miracle.

A key remark that Jesus made to his mother gives us a hint at what he was thinking and why he chose to make this event the scene for his first miracle. When his mother asked him to intervene, Jesus said to her, "My hour has not yet come."

What was he talking about?

Jesus, as he often did, was talking from a spiritual vantage point. He was talking about *his* wedding. Jesus had come to earth as a loving bridegroom to take a bride for himself from among the sons and daughters of the human race. But the hour for his wedding had not yet arrived. When it does come, however, the food at his wedding banquet will be plentiful, and the wine will be exotic and will never run out. It will be better tasting wine than any palate on earth has ever experienced.

What you can learn from this story is this: Jesus is full of grace for the undeserving. Jesus can miraculously turn ordinary water into extraordinary wine. He can take ordinary vessels, like you and me, and fill us up with his life. His life is like the best of wines that makes the heart glad. This is the wine of joy, something that people in this world desperately long for. Jesus wants to fill us with this wine, and then pour it out to others through us.

CLEANSING OF THE TEMPLE

CHAPTER 2

John recorded two stories in the second chapter of his gospel—the first was the wedding in Cana, which we discussed yesterday, and the second was about Jesus' cleansing of the Temple. Though on the surface there may seem to be no connection between these two stories, as you read on, I think you'll find an explanation for why John puts them together in this order.

First, a little background to this story:

This is the first of two times recorded in the gospels where Jesus cleansed the Temple. This occasion in John took place at the very beginning of Jesus' public ministry, shortly after the miracle at Cana of Galilee, probably in April of 27 A.D. The second time it occurred was three years later, just after his triumphal entry into Jerusalem before he was crucified.

John began this story with, "The Passover of the Jews was at hand." Before we get into the Temple cleansing, I want to pull over for a minute here to explain the Passover.

Three times a year Jews came from all over the Roman Empire to Jerusalem to offer sacrifices and pay their taxes to support the Temple. The Passover feast was one of those three annual celebrations and took place sometime in March or April, according to our calendar.

Another one of those feasts was the Harvest Festival, also known as Pentecost. Pentecost means "Fiftieth" because it took place exactly fifty days after Passover. This happened sometime in late May or June, commemorating the summer harvest.

Finally, there was the Festival of Ingathering, also known as the Feast of Booths or Tabernacles. This occurred toward the end of the year, in late September to mid-October. There were other feasts and celebrations as well, but these were the three main ones.

The first Passover celebration occurred some 1,300 to 1,500 years earlier, the night before Moses led the Hebrew people out of Egypt, where they were enslaved, to take them to the land of promise. After multiple warnings, Pharaoh had continued to resist Moses' demands to let God's people go. Finally, each family was instructed to slay a lamb and put the blood on the doorposts of their homes. Then God sent the death angel to take the life of every first-born son in Egypt. Only the lives of those who had the blood of the lamb on their doorposts were spared.

It is not insignificant that Jesus was crucified at the time of the Passover feast in 30 A.D. Just as the Hebrew people in the Exodus story were covered by "the blood of the lamb" and passed from death to life, so too the blood of Christ, our Passover lamb, has delivered us from death and brought us into life.

For the Jews, Passover marked the end of their time in slavery and their birth as the Hebrew nation. Moses even gave them a new calendar and way to number their months, beginning with the month of the Passover.

For us, Passover also represents a new beginning. Believing in Jesus as our Passover Lamb is the starting point of the Christian life. The Apostle Paul latched onto this truth well when he wrote his second letter to a group of believers in Corinth saying that anyone who is in Christ is a new creature; old things have passed away and new things have come (2 Corinthians 5:17).

On that very first Passover, the children of Israel had to leave Egypt quickly. They did not have time for their bread to rise, so they made it in haste, without leaven (yeast). Consequently, this festival is also known as the Festival of Unleavened Bread.

With that explanation of the Passover behind us, we can merge once more into John's account of the cleansing of the Temple.

The Jews, coming from all over the world, couldn't bring their sheep and cattle with them. They needed to buy the animals for sacrifice in Jerusalem. If they bought the animals elsewhere, there was no guarantee that the priests would approve of them.

Why was that? This was not only a convenient way of doing things. The priests had exploited and corrupted the sacrificial rites, turning them into a moneymaking business. They formed an alliance with the animal merchants and, in collaboration with them, profited off the system. This became accepted practice.

In addition, people came to Jerusalem to pay tribute (the Temple tax). The tax they paid had to be made in shekels (Temple currency), so they had to change their money with moneychangers. These moneychangers took a percentage and shared the profit with, once again—guess who— the priests.

What was supposed to be the Father's house had become a bazaar. Greediness and exploitation, like a cancer, had taken root and metastasized, corrupting the whole system. That day, Jesus went into the Temple with a whip made of small ropes, drove them all out, poured out the coins, and overturned their tables.

The priests asked by what authority he had done this. Their authority had been challenged, and their interests exposed and disrupted. Jesus responded on another level, with a heavenly truth that they did not comprehend. He said, "Destroy this temple, and in three days I will raise it up" (John 2:19). The temple he was referring to was the temple of his body, because the Spirit of God resided in him.

Jesus was leading them down the rabbit hole again, just as Morpheus led Neo to a new reality by giving him the red pill. There was another temple that they knew nothing about. Jesus was telling them that the Temple in Jerusalem, made of stone, was only a replica, part of the Matrix. It was not real. He was the real temple that *their* temple was supposed to represent. Not only was Jesus the real temple, but once he comes into our lives and takes up residence, we become temples as well.

Jesus' actions here demonstrated his zeal to overturn all idols that distract and keep people from worshiping the true and living God (an idol is any person or thing that people admire or love more than God). In this case it was money. But it goes beyond that. Jesus wants to remove any corruption, any false religious concepts and practices, and any misconceptions that come between us and the God we were created to worship. This event also fulfilled a prophecy concerning Jesus from Psalm 69:9: "For zeal for Your house has consumed me."

Lest we be too quick to point the finger and condemn those leading priests and moneychangers, we must direct the question at ourselves: where do we need Jesus to overturn the tables in our own lives? Where do we need him to remove the idols that compete with him, expose the corruption, and tear down our own misconceptions?

In the first story in chapter 2 we saw that Jesus' plan was to have a bride, but his hour had not yet come. Now we see him cleansing the Temple. If we are to be prepared and made ready to meet our Bridegroom, surely this cleansing will need to take place in our own lives as well.

Something to ponder...

GRACE FOR THE MOST RELIGIOUS: NICODEMUS AND THE NEW BIRTH

CHAPTER 3

I hope that since our last coffee time together you have continued to ponder this concept of Jesus cleansing the temple. We are each a temple. It's not for me to point out areas in your life that may need to change, or for you to point out areas in mine. That is God's job. That is the work of the Holy Spirit to do.

Jesus will not force himself on anyone. We were created with free wills and God honors our prerogative to choose—to accept him or reject him. Without freedom of choice, there can be no true love.

But God also honors the desires of our hearts. If we pray to him sincerely, he will respond. If we desire to follow him, to love him more, and to be changed to become more like him, he will honor these kinds of prayers. So if there are things in your life that you perceive the Lord is pointing out that he wants to change, talk with him about it. Give him the green light. He doesn't work on us to punish us, but to set us free.

Moving on to chapter 3, John next draws our attention to Jesus' dealings with one of the most religious men in all of Israel—Nicodemus. Nicodemus had risen to the highest position of prominence among the Jews and was among the most knowledgeable in Jewish law and tradition. Yet Jesus perceived that, on the inside, Nicodemus was empty and came to him because he had the heart of a seeker, desiring truth. And Jesus did not turn him away.

The disciples were common folk. They were made up of fishermen, a tax collector (who the Jews naturally hated), a zealot (who was full-on committed to not paying taxes to Rome—I'm sure those two butted heads often!), one serious doubter and skeptic, and others of similar dubious background. They were a crusty, crude, down-to-earth bunch. They saw the hypocrisy of the Pharisees and despised their religiosity. They witnessed how these religious leaders paraded around in their costumes, prayed and fasted to be noticed by others, and sat at the chief spots at the religious feasts and social gatherings. They would probably have stood up and cheered when John the Baptizer called the Pharisees a brood of snakes and vipers on the day the religious leaders came out to see him baptizing in the Jordan River. They probably would have viewed Nicodemus with a high degree of skepticism and suspicion—if not distain—if they had heard that he wanted an audience with Jesus.

Nicodemus began the conversation with Jesus with some praise for him, acknowledging that he had come from God, was a great teacher, and that God must be with him because of the continual signs he was performing.

But before he could get any further and even ask Jesus a question, Jesus responded to him in such a shocking way that it was like hitting him in the head with a shovel.

Jesus' words were sharp, crisp, and forceful: "Nicodemus, if you have any hope for ever seeing the kingdom of God, you are going to need to be born all over again" (my paraphrase). Not a very complementary or respectful thing to say to one of the greatest teachers in Israel!

After a probable nervous adjustment of his turban and clearing of his throat, Nicodemus, obviously puzzled, asked something like this, "What do you mean? How can a person enter into his mother's womb after being born and get a do-over? How is that supposed to happen?"

Once again, as so frequently occurred, while Nicodemus was speaking from an earthly, human perspective, Jesus was speaking of a deeper, truer reality. He took this opportunity to dispense a red pill of truth to Nicodemus. Jesus said, "Truly, truly, I say to you, unless one is born of water and the Spirit he cannot enter into the kingdom of God" (John 3:5).

Jesus told Nicodemus that the first birth, which every person experiences, occurs upon entry into this world from a sack of water in the womb. This is a birth of which we have no choice. But the second birth does involve a choice and is activated by our faith (believing). It is a birth by the Spirit that delivers us not into this world, but into the kingdom of God.

Every birth involves coming out of darkness and receiving a new life. At human birth we received human life. At the second birth we receive divine life—the *zoe* life of God. (Remember our discussion of this word earlier?) Entering the kingdom of God is not, as Nicodemus supposed, a matter of acquiring some new religious teaching. It is a matter of receiving a new *life*!

That day, Jesus revealed that the grace of God extends to even the most religious people, if they have open hearts. The truth that we learn through the story of Nicodemus is that behind every human birth there is a bigger heavenly reality. Jesus wants us to experience the *new* birth that comes from receiving a *new life* from the Spirit, which will introduce us to a whole new realm in which to live—the kingdom of God.

How to Receive the New Birth

CHAPTER 3

Thank God for Nicodemus. Thank God that he was a seeker and that he persisted in asking questions. The answers Jesus gave him not only helped him, but help us as well.

Jesus told Nicodemus that in order for him to see the kingdom of God, he needed to be born again. Then Jesus proceeded to tell him that the second birth was a spiritual birth. Just like the first birth, the second birth involves receiving a new life—a life from above. One needed to be born of the Spirit if they were ever to enter into the realm of the Spirit, which is the realm of the kingdom of God.

That was new and important information for Nicodemus to process and assimilate, but it didn't answer an important question: how? How can a person do that? How can one experience that second birth? So Nicodemus asked once again, "How can these things be?"

Praise God that Jesus didn't leave Nicodemus in the dark. He referred him back to a story from the Book of Numbers that Nicodemus was well acquainted with. Nicodemus had committed this story to memory because he was a Pharisee. As a Pharisee, it was required of all Pharisees that they memorize the first five books of the Jewish Bible, the Torah. The story came from Numbers 21:4-9:

> ...the people grew impatient on the way; they spoke against God and against Moses, and said, "Why have you brought us up out of Egypt to die in the wilderness? There is no bread! There is no water! And we detest this miserable food!"
>
> Then the Lord sent venomous snakes among them; they bit the people and many Israelites died. The people came to Moses and said, "We sinned when we spoke against the Lord and against you. Pray that the Lord will take the snakes away from us." So Moses prayed for the people.
>
> The Lord said to Moses, "Make a snake and put it up on a pole; anyone who is bitten can look at it and live." So Moses made a bronze snake and put it up on a pole. Then when anyone was bitten by a snake and looked at the bronze snake, they lived. N I V

This was Jesus' answer to the "how" question.

He told Nicodemus, "As Moses lifted up the serpent in the wilderness, even so the Son of Man must be lifted up; so that whoever believers in Him will have eternal life" (John 3:14-15).

The people in the wilderness were complaining against God and Moses. (They were always complaining!) The wilderness was a difficult place. They were tired of the long journey. And they were tired of the food God was providing. They always seemed to be complaining about the food! They were even considering aborting the trip and returning to slavery in Egypt because they weren't getting the fish, cucumbers, melons, leeks, onions, and garlic that they were used to.

God disciplined them for complaining and sent poisonous snakes into the camp. (Some translations refer to them as "fiery serpents" because of the burning sensation one would experience when bitten.) As a result, a number of people died. They realized that they had sinned against God and against Moses, so they asked Moses to pray for them. He did.

God told Moses to make a bronze snake, lift it up on a pole, and those who looked at the snake would live. Bronze in the Bible typically represents judgment. The snake typically represents the Satan or sin.

What Jesus was essentially saying to Nicodemus was this: Nicodemus, do you want to know how to be born again and receive a new life so that you can enter the kingdom of God? Well, here's how. Just like those Israelites who sinned had to look at that bronze snake that was lifted up on the pole in order to live, you are going to have to look to me.

Since the fall of Adam, everyone in this world has received Satan's poisonous, deadly snakebite. The whole human race is sin-infected and, as a result, destined to die. What happened to those Israelites in the wilderness was an illustration for you to learn from. I am going to be lifted up on the cross. God is going to place upon me the sin of the entire world. I am going to take upon myself the sin nature of the snake and become that snake, and there on the cross the snake is going to be judged. I am going to take upon myself the penalty for sin that you deserved and die in your place, so that you will not have to die.

You ask, how can one be born again? I'll tell you plainly. Look to me.

Believe in me. Believe that what I have done on the cross is for you. Only then will you be healed from your snakebite and live. By looking to me and believing, you will enter a new reality and receive the eternal life that I have promised.

Dear Friend, if you are reading this and you are not already a Christian, this would be a good opportunity for you to receive Jesus right now. He came to save you from your sin and offer you the free gift of eternal life. Invite him into your life right now. A simple prayer is all you need:

Dear Lord Jesus,

I want to know you. Come into my life. Forgive me of my sins. Be my Lord.

Give me that new life that you promised. Amen.

JESUS MUST INCREASE, WE MUST DECREASE

CHAPTER 3

So glad to be with you again!

I've been sharing some pretty heavy stuff with you these last few days, ever since we launched our actual study on the Book of John. I want to introduce some new material today, but before I do, I think it would be a good idea to do a little review.

Sometimes in the quest for knowledge or truth things can seem very complicated. But truth is always simple. God loves everyone, from the least to the greatest, from the dumbest to the smartest. That's why God needed to have a way that people from across the spectrum could relate to him.

The Bible teaches that our salvation is not works-based—a result of human effort. It is faith-based. Here's why: if it were works-based, God would need to be counting our failures and comparing us to others, so that we would all be judged on the same system. If one person committed 110,999,999 sins against God, and the next person committed one more, tallying 111,000,000, and if 111 million was the cut-off point, would it really be fair for God to welcome the first into the kingdom, and cut off the second?

Or does God's mercy operate on a sliding scale? If a person dies at age twenty, are they allotted so many sins to commit, while at eighty, a person is allowed four times that amount?

None of this, of course, represents an accurate assessment of how God relates to humankind. God had to have a way for everyone—from the most brilliant to the least intelligent, from the strongest and healthiest to those with physical hindrances or limitations—to access him. God chose faith (believing) as the common point of entry for all. That's why God rewards those with faith like a little child. And that's why truth can and should to be presented and understood in the simplest of terms.

That's what I'm going to try to do now: I'm going to review and summarize what has been presented thus far at its most basic level. By doing so, I think that you will see that John was not being random by ordering his book the way he does.

CHAPTER 1:

- Jesus was God.
- Jesus lived in another realm—a heavenly, spiritual realm with his Father.
- Jesus came to earth and took the form of a man.
- Jesus was the Lamb of God, who came to die to take away the sin of the world.
- Jesus began to call people to follow him: to be part of his kingdom.
- That kingdom consists of men and women, boys and girls, from every people group, tribe, and nation.

- Jesus is the undisputed king in this kingdom.
- Jesus was not only fully, 100 percent God, but he was also fully, 100 percent man—both Son of God and Son of Man.

CHAPTER 2:

- Jesus came seeking a bride who he could love and who would love him in return.
- In order for us to become that bride, we need to undergo a cleansing.

CHAPTER 3:

- The starting point of our relationship with Jesus is the second birth through which we receive the divine life by faith (believing).
- It is only through this second birth that we can see or enter into the realm that Jesus came from and that he wants for us to co-inhabit with him.
- The reality from which Jesus comes casts a shadow here on the earth. Many of the things we see with our eyes are only pictures, shadows, or images of the true reality of God.

OK so far?

Now, what's the next thing John wants us to see?

Next, our attention is directed to John the Baptizer once again. John's disciples had come to John and asked him who this other person was who was also baptizing people and attracting large crowds.

John answered curiously but profoundly. He said that the other person (Jesus) was the Bridegroom, and that he (John) was only a friend of the Bridegroom.

Did he really know what he was saying? Did he really comprehend that Jesus had come for a bride? Maybe he did, but maybe he only understood in part.

At that point, this prophet dressed in camel skin gave us another insight into how the bride of Christ would be made ready for her kingly Bridegroom. John said, "He must increase, but I must decrease."

Receiving new life from Jesus is the starting point. Then, a transformative process begins to take place in which the life of Christ grows and manifests itself within us. This is the path to spiritual maturity.

John then told us the way in which this will occur. This will be accomplished through the working of the Spirit that will be given without measure.

I don't know about you, but this makes me just want to praise God! By grace we have each been called to follow Jesus. By grace and by his Spirit working in and through us, Jesus will increase in us, we will decrease, and we will be made more and more like him!

He's taken the initiative and responsibility for it all.

The good news keeps getting better, doesn't it?

GRACE FOR THE GREATEST OF SINNERS: THE SAMARITAN WOMAN

CHAPTER 4

If God can extend grace to the most religious people, like Nicodemus, who exert every effort to keep the rules and earn their salvation, then what about those on the opposite end of the scale? How far does the grace of God reach to the greatest sinners? To answer that question, the Holy Spirit placed Jesus' encounter with the Samaritan woman at the well next in the sequence of the stories presented in the Book of John.

The Samaritans were a group of people who lived in Samaria, an area north of Jerusalem. They were half-breeds—half-Jews and half-Gentiles. Some 750 years earlier, when most of the Jews in Palestine were taken captive into Babylon, some were left behind. Those Jews intermarried with the Assyrians. Over time, the Samaritans constructed their own temple, in opposition to the Temple in Jerusalem. Thus, they were neither fully Jews nor fully Gentiles (Gentiles are all non-Jews).

This was a day Jesus broke all the rules of proper conduct for a Jew. It was midday. His disciples had gone to town to purchase some food and left Jesus alone at Jacob's well. Jacob was one of the Patriarchs in Old Testament times. His father was Isaac, and his grandfather was Abraham.

When the disciples returned, they found Jesus talking with a Samaritan woman. They were shocked because this seemed like indecorous, if not scandalous, behavior. For a rabbi (a Jewish religious scholar or teacher, which Jesus was) to be found alone with a woman was not something any good rabbi would do.

But she was not only a woman, she was a Samaritan woman, and the Jews had nothing to do with Samaritans. Think of this in terms of the stereotypical relationships between German Nazis and Jews, Turks and Armenians, or the Hutus and the Tutsis. That's what we're talking about here.

Furthermore, she was not only a Samaritan, but she was known to be a very sinful woman. She had five husbands previously and was currently living with a man to whom she was not married. She was a woman beyond shame and callously indifferent to what anyone thought of her.

But Jesus saw that this woman was broken inside. She was an empty shell of one who was created to bear God's image, with great needs and a deep hunger for something satisfying and real. She had been through so many relationships and disappointments, thinking that in them she would find the happiness that she longed for. But time after time she came up empty.

Jesus spoke to her, disregarding the social customs and barriers. The living waters from his spirit flowed into her and satisfied her soul like nothing she had ever known before.

He told her that if she drank of the water that he had to give her, she would never thirst again. Those waters would become a well of eternal life within her to spring up and refresh her thirsty soul.

I'd like to stop for a moment and ask you a question just to drive home the point Jesus was making.

Do you normally order a glass of water with your coffee when you drink it, to help with hydration? Or bring a water bottle along? I'm assuming you do. Could I ask you please to pick up that glass of water and look at it? Now tell me, what's inside the glass? Water, right? Think again! What you are looking at is a picture, a shadow, a replica, an imitation of water.

The Samaritan woman was next in line in John's Gospel to swallow the red pill of truth. Living on this earth, it is impossible to survive without water. Three days max. Jesus said that the water from Jacob's well—or any well—would never satisfy. She'd need to keep coming back over and over and over again. But the water he had to offer her was different. That water was *alive.* Only Jesus could give her water that was alive, and he *was* that water!

If Jesus is going to increase in you, you need to learn to drink of him. You need to take that red pill for yourself and see the new reality. Ask Jesus to make this truth real for you. You can drink of him because through the new birth, God's Spirit has come to live inside of you. He is like a fresh spring of water that will bubble up within you to transform your soul with the eternal life that you have received. This, too, is a gift of God, a product of pure grace!

Every day, when you get up in the morning and fill your water glass, Jesus is giving you one more opportunity to be reminded of who he is and what he wants to be for you.

Lift your glass to Jesus! Give him a shout out, or just thank him that he's made his life so accessible to you—just like drinking a simple glass of water!

DAY 23

MORE REVELATION FOR THE SAMARITAN WOMAN: WHERE TO WORSHIP

CHAPTER 4

I want to come back to the story of the Samaritan woman again this morning. Jesus spent a lot of time with that woman that day. Besides learning that Jesus had water to give her that was alive and would quench the thirst of her parched soul, Jesus used this occasion to reveal to her another amazing truth. That truth was about worship.

The Samaritans had their temple on Mount Gerizim. The Jews had theirs in Jerusalem. The woman perceived that Jesus was a prophet when he hacked her email and revealed that he knew all about her—that she had been married five times and that the guy she was currently living with hadn't even bothered to give her a ring.

Wanting to appear informed and show Jesus that she knew a thing or two about religion, or perhaps feeling embarrassed and wanting to change the subject, she asked him a question. Basically, it was this: Who's got it right? You Jews say that Jerusalem is where we're supposed to worship

God. We Samaritans say it is here at Mount Gerizim. You are a prophet. Which is it?

Her question pertained to location—this mountain or that one. Jesus' answer also pertained to location, but not in the way she was expecting. It's not about this mountain or that mountain, Jesus said: "But an hour is coming, and now is, when the true [real] worshipers will worship the Father in spirit and truth [reality]; for such people the Father seeks to be His worshipers. God is spirit, and those who worship Him must worship in spirit and truth [reality]" (John 4:23-24).

People have had it in their heads since who-knows-when that in order to worship you need to go to a building somewhere. Not so.

Jesus had the eternal Father God living inside of him. He didn't need to go anywhere to worship God. God was right there with him. God lived in him—in his spirit. This was a locatable place. He could go to his spirit any time to worship the living God.

Here's some more information that will help make this clear.

The Old Testament Temple, which was built, then rebuilt because it was destroyed once, was in Jerusalem. God had given David the blueprint to build it, and his son, Solomon, had overseen its construction. The Temple had three parts—an outer court, an inner court, and the Holy of Holies. The Holy of Holies was where God lived. I won't describe that building for you now, or the significance of all that was in it. The important thing pertaining to this discussion is that it had three parts.

Elsewhere in the Bible, the Apostle Paul taught that we humans are also made up of three parts—body, soul, and spirit. (See Paul's first letter to the Thessalonians, chapter five, verse twenty-three, if you want to look this up.) God created us with bodies so that we could contact and interact with the physical world, souls so we could contact and interact with other people, and spirits so that we could contact and interact with God.

I don't need to explain to you what our bodies are—that's pretty self-evident.

Our souls are our personalities, who we are—each one of us is a unique individual. We have minds to think, emotions to feel, wills to make decisions.

Our spirits are the third component of who we are. If I could point to a location where you could find (or sense) that spirit, it would not be in your head, but somewhere inside your rib cage. It is the essence in us that makes us able to commune with God, like a "spiritual heart."

Before we made the decision to follow Christ, our spirits were dead to God. But then we invited Jesus to come into our lives, and he did. Since he is Spirit, where do you think he came to reside? In our spirits! His Spirit joined to our spirits. That's where Jesus is now!

When Jesus said, "The hour is coming, and now is, when true [real] worshippers would worship the Father in spirit and in truth [reality]," he could say the hour *now is*, because *he* was doing it that way. He was worshipping the Father in his spirit. The hour was also *coming*, because very soon, people like the Samaritan woman and you and me would be worshipping that way also!

This is great news!

Isn't it wonderful that Jesus is not walking around somewhere on this earth today as he was before his crucifixion and resurrection? If he were, we'd have to hop a flight and get on a plane to be with him where he was in order to worship him. But now, because he was raised from the dead, and his Spirit has come to live in us, we can be with him and worship him at any time and in any place!

What a wonderful plan to make worship accessible for all! I'm so glad that Jesus is there with you right now and that you can worship him any time you want to!

DAY 24

THE SAMARITAN WOMAN: ANOTHER NOBODY THAT BECAME A SOMEBODY

CHAPTER 4

Let's take one parting glance at that fortunate Samaritan woman before her story fades and slips off the pages of the Bible. Once Jesus was raised from the dead, the apostles and others went out from Jerusalem to Samaria and other parts of Israel to preach the good news about Jesus. There is no doubt in my mind that a new church (a gathering of believers—not a building) formed in her city, and that this woman had become a real worshipper, worshipping God in spirit and in reality, along with those other Samaritans that had spent time with Jesus for those two days.

This woman came to Jesus with an empty bucket, but walked away with water that was alive.

She came to him as a miserable failure, rejected by society, but she left accepted by God.

She came hopeless, but left with hope.

She came as one with questions, but left with answers for others.

The same wonderful changes take place in our lives every time we encounter Jesus.

She was also the first one that Jesus actually told, directly, that he was the Messiah.

And, she is a wonderful illustration of the bride Jesus came to seek and to find. She was a half-breed, part Jew and part Gentile—just like the church. She was a sinful woman who believed in him, was made part of his bride, and loved him with a passion.

The earthly Temple in Jerusalem where people came to worship God was only a picture, a shadow, and no longer necessary. That temple had served its purpose. It was even necessary that it be destroyed in 70 A.D., because had it remained standing, it would have been a distraction. Jesus ushered in a whole new era, where old things passed away, and new things had come.

Another thing we can learn from this story is that once this woman received the revelation of who Jesus was, she became his ambassador. Through her, the message of the gospel spread. Jesus saw those Samaritans that she had talked to from her village coming to him—walking that dusty road from their village to the well—as sheaves of wheat, ready to be harvested. That woman became one of Jesus' co-laborers that he used in the real harvest, the harvest of souls.

Finally, I'd like to point out one last thing about Jesus in this story. The story began with Jesus being tired and hungry. The disciples went to the village to buy food. By the time they returned, they found him deep in conversation with this woman. When she left to go back to her village, they offered him bread, but Jesus told them that he had food to eat that they didn't know anything about. His food was to do the will of his Father and the work the Father had given him to do.

There is earthly food that satisfies, but there is also food that comes from knowing God; this spiritual food is so satisfying we can even lose our physical appetites. Jesus lived in another realm and constantly ate of that heavenly food to give him strength. But he also lived among us, and ate the bread mortals eat. He was the God-man, at home in the world from which he came, and at home in the world that he created.

I encourage you to worship him today, wherever you are or wherever you go. The Father is looking for true worshippers who worship like this!

Grace for the Powerful & the Wealthy: The Healing of the Rich Man's Son

CHAPTER 4

Good morning! Ready to take in some more?

So far, we have seen Jesus touch the lives of all kinds of people: one really weird dude (you know who that was), businessmen (the fishermen that he called to follow him), the undeserving, those whose lives needed to be cleaned up, one of the most religious men of Israel, one of the most sinful women, and now we come to the story at the end of John chapter four where Jesus healed a royal official's son.

It's a rather short story, but there are a number of things we can learn here.

This was the second sign, or miracle, that Jesus performed. This also took place in Cana of Galilee where his first miracle—the turning of the water into wine—had occurred. Cana was just a short distance from Nazareth where Jesus grew up.

This miracle involved the healing of a royal official's son who had a high fever and was at the point of death.

This man lived in Capernaum. During the Roman Empire, to be a "royal" official meant that this was a man of prominence and wealth. We read in this passage, for instance, that the man owned slaves—probably a number of them.

However, this man's prominence and wealth were of no use to him in this time of crisis. As a wealthy man, he probably could have afforded the best doctors. But they were unable to heal the boy. He had run out of options. Only Jesus was left.

At this point the official was desperate. It looked like all hope was gone, so he left the dying boy in his bed and struck out on a twenty-mile, seven-hour trek to go find Jesus.

He had in mind that Jesus needed to return to Capernaum with him to heal his son. But Jesus doesn't always do things according to our plans.

Jesus told the man to go home because his son would live.

Turning water to wine was a great miracle. But this! This wasn't just avoiding embarrassment at a wedding reception. This was a life and death event! Not only could Jesus perform miracles when he was physically present with people, but he could perform miracles on those who were miles away.

Here John reveals Jesus to us as the ever-present, all-seeing God. Jesus could be at Cana talking with the man, but at the same time be at the boy's bedside in Spirit in Capernaum, healing him! This is easier for us to understand today because Jesus is no longer confined to a physical body but is in Spirit, and now miracles around the globe can occur simultaneously where Jesus can be in many places at the same time.

Is your understanding of who Jesus is beginning to grow? I certainly hope so!

This should also give you confidence when you pray. You don't need to be present with that sick relative in another state, our President in his office at the White House, or that foreign missionary overseas. Jesus is in you; Jesus is there; he can hear, and he can answer.

There was another point Jesus made in connection with this story.

Jesus said that a prophet had no honor in his own country. At this point in Jesus' ministry, when he had just returned from the Passover feast, the Galileans received him because they saw the things he had done in Jerusalem. They must also have seen, or heard of, the first miracle in Cana, for he was back there again. There was interest in Jesus—even from the hometown crowd—as long as he was performing miracles.

But Jesus did not come to earth just to be a magician.

Following the royal official's plea for Jesus to heal his son, Jesus' immediate answer to him was a curious one. He remarked that unless the man saw signs and wonders he would not believe. Why did Jesus say this?

Jesus knew this man's heart. He knew that if he did not answer his prayer, if he let his son die, this man would never believe in Jesus. The official might have had some hope, but desperation drove him more than faith. So Jesus spoke a word, and the man walked away believing.

This is your God. He is full of grace and truth. Jesus had grace for this man. He wanted to help him in his unbelief. And he wants to help you in yours.

But what happens when we pray and our prayers are not answered? Do we, like those Galileans, need to see miracles in order to believe in Jesus? Or can we just believe his word without seeing a sign, and then go on our way?

John's former business partner, close friend, and fellow apostle, Peter, was a man of faith. He was also known to have had the gift of healing. In one of his letters, Peter said that our faith would be tested. Once it has been tested and refined, it will prove to be much more valuable than gold and will result in praise, glory, and honor when Jesus reveals himself. But Peter also said that even though we don't see Jesus, we still love him, and that just by believing, we will have great joy.

Since Peter had the gift of healing, does that mean he saw Jesus heal every person that he prayed for? We don't know. But that is not the experience of most Christians. Whether it is praying for people to be healed or circumstances to change, the fact is that sometimes we just don't see immediate answers to our prayers. Maybe it is timing. Perhaps there are things in difficult circumstances that God wants for us or for those we are praying for to learn.

When it comes to praying for others, or even for ourselves, some of the bad situations we find ourselves in are simply the result of poor choices. Choices have consequences. Other bad situations can originate from demonic activity or from accidents or someone else's negligence. Still others can come from sickness or disease, which are just the results of living in a fallen world. But if we pray and don't see immediate results, that should not deter us from praying. Sometimes it's just difficult to know how to pray.

Oftentimes, the way we want to see God do things does not conform to the way he wants to do them. (Like the wealthy man wanting Jesus to make a special trip to Capernaum.) That's why we need to learn how to pray. When you pray in certain circumstances, you'll need to ask God for discernment to pray according to his will. The New Testament teaches us to continually pray. Why? Prayer is not solely for the purpose of getting answers. Prayer is for the purpose of relationship! God wants us to talk with him, so he can talk with us.

The apostle Paul was no stranger to being in difficult circumstances. In 2 Corinthians 12:8-9 he wrote about how he prayed three times that God would remove a burdensome, painful situation in his life, but God's response was, "My grace is sufficient for you, for power is perfected in weakness." This prompted him to write, "Most gladly, therefore, I will rather boast about my weaknesses, so that the power of Christ may dwell in me. Therefore I am well content with weaknesses, with insults, with distresses, with persecutions, with difficulties, for Christ's sake; for when I am weak, then I am strong."

Through his difficult circumstances and even unanswered prayer, Paul learned to be content and that God was enough.

If you see miracles when you pray, praise God! If you don't see a miracle or a healing right away, don't let that discourage you. Ask God to show you how you can pray more effectively. Recognize that there could be a higher purpose involved by God not answering your prayers the way you think they should be answered. Believing God's word, and leaving things with Jesus, trusting in his all-sufficiency rather than requiring miracles to believe, will lead you to praise him and love him. And that will result in joy, regardless of the outcomes.

Grace for the Helpless: The Healing of the Invalid at the Pool of Bethesda

CHAPTER 5

We're now in chapter 5 of our journey through the Book of John. It begins with the story of an invalid man that Jesus healed.

Just outside of the Temple in Jerusalem was a place for ritual bathing called the Pool of Bethesda. Bethesda means "house of mercy" or "place of flowing water." Here, multitudes of the infirm would gather, hoping for a miracle by which they would be healed.

One of those people was an invalid man who had been in his helpless condition for thirty-eight years. If Jesus were in the business of trying to recruit an army of able-bodied followers to help usher in his kingdom, this man was certainly no likely candidate. He had nothing to offer. He was not an influential member of the community; he was not a "key kid on campus." He was no one of standing or position. He had few, if any, friends. He was insignificant in terms of how society measures people.

But Jesus performed a miracle and healed this man because Jesus saw value in him. He had value not because of what he could offer Jesus, but because this man was God's creation, his precious child, and for that reason alone he was worthy.

The grace that Jesus poured out upon him was not dependent on what the man could give back in return. If we could all clearly understand the grace of God, we would see that we are all like this man. God did not choose us because of how good we are or because of what we have to offer him. Grace is extended to each of us solely on the basis of Jesus' unconditional love.

This story shows—as do all the stories in John's Gospel—how frequently the disciples witnessed their teacher committing seemingly random, mind-blowing, unreasonable, unmerited, inconceivable acts of grace and mercy. Those acts of grace and mercy made deep impressions on those men and they were changed themselves as a result.

Jesus also used this man and this healing to highlight another spiritual reality. The infirm people lying around Bethesda's pool represented the condition of those within Judaism. Like these infirm, those relying on religious myths and misconceptions, waiting for something to happen to make them whole, were most often disappointed. The helpless man said to Jesus, "Sir, I have no man to put me into the pool when the water is stirred up, but while I am coming, another steps down before me" (John 5:7). He was trusting in the religious superstition that an angel might come and stir the waters, and if he were the first one to get into the water, he might be healed. However, standing before him was the "real" Bethesda, the heavenly source of flowing waters who had the capacity to heal.

It was no coincidence John noted that this man had been in his condition for thirty-eight years. To find out why the Holy Spirit chose this man as an illustration for John to write about, we need to go back and examine an episode from Israel's history.

From the time the Israelites left Egypt to the time they entered the land of Canaan was 40 years. Upon their departure from Egypt, they went to a place called Sinai and encamped there for about a year. That was where Moses received the law in an encounter with God and where they first built their Tabernacle. (The Tabernacle was God's portable dwelling place—a tent—that God came to live in from the time of the exodus until the conquest of Canaan, when the people finally erected a permanent temple in Jerusalem).

Then they left Sinai and marched for eleven days to another desert outpost called Kadesh Barnea, at the southern border of the Promised Land.

From there, they sent twelve spies in to check out the Promised Land. The spies came back with a mixed report. Two of them, Caleb and Joshua, who saw that it was a good land, filled with milk and honey and abundant fruit, wanted to immediately go in and take the land. They were confident that, even though there were enemies in the land, the God who delivered them from Pharaoh and his army, the God who worked miracles, would deliver them from these enemies.

The other ten spies did not give a favorable report. They were afraid to go in because they thought those enemies were too strong and would overpower them. When the rest of the people heard this negative report, they became fearful as well. They reasoned that they would be killed in battle and that their wives and children would be captured. They wanted to choose a new leader in place of Moses, and go back to Egypt.

God was angry with that generation because of their unbelief and said they would not enter the land. This resulted in their wandering around in the wilderness for another thirty-eight years (Deuteronomy 2:14), until the entire generation of adults over twenty years of age had died off, and a new generation was raised up that could trust God. Then he would take *them* into the land.

The fact that this invalid was crippled for thirty-eight years would have immediately caught the attention of any Jewish reader. Those Jews who had wandered the wilderness were also spiritual cripples for thirty-eight years because of their unbelief. Thus, this man represented the paralyzing unbelief of all those who remain in Judaism (or the world) and end up getting nowhere. Apart from trusting in Christ, they could not be made whole; apart from Christ, there was no deliverance or healing.

The Jewish leaders objected that Jesus healed this man on the Sabbath. This exposed their distorted thinking. To them, it was better for a person to remain spiritually dead and physically handicapped than to break a single religious rule.

By including this story in his narrative, John continued to diversify the many types of people whose lives Jesus touched. Add this helpless man to our former list of those impacted by Jesus—businessmen, the undeserving, the corrupt and self-serving, the religious, the most sinful, the weird, the wealthy and prominent—and we see that Jesus extends his love to every type of person. Somewhere within that messy spectrum of humanity, you probably see yourself. If Jesus' grace was sufficient for these kinds of people, surely he can meet you right where you are under any circumstance as well!

Jesus: the Example for Living the Christian Life

CHAPTER 5

Like the other stories we've looked at so far, multiple spiritual lessons and principles can be extracted from the story of the invalid man. So we're going to spend some more time on it today. One of the revelations that we find in this story is actually one of the greatest insights to be found anywhere on how the Christian life is intended to be lived.

Jesus is the model Christian. He is the prototype for all Christians. He was the perfect God-man. What was his secret for being able to do miracles, teach with such authority, and live the extraordinary way he lived?

Here it is, in his words:

> I assure you: The Son is not able to do anything on
> His own, but only what He sees the Father doing. For
> whatever the Father does, the Son also does these things
> in the same way. For the Father loves the Son and shows

> Him everything He is doing, and He will show Him
> greater works than these so that you will be amazed.
>
> JOHN 5:19-20HCSB

Later, in John 12:49-50 he said,

> For I did not speak on My own initiative, but the Father
> Himself who sent Me has given Me a commandment *as
> to* what to say and what to speak. I know that His com-
> mandment is eternal life; therefore the things I speak, I
> speak just as the Father has told Me.

Jesus' secret for living the Christian life was that he only did the things he saw his Father doing, and spoke the things he heard his Father speaking! How could this be?

The Bible teaches us that Jesus' miraculous conception was the result of the Holy Spirit coming upon the Virgin Mary and impregnating her. No human father was involved in that conception. Jesus' human life came from his mother, Mary. But within him, Jesus possessed a treasure that no human being that had ever lived before him possessed. Living within Jesus' spirit was the divine life of the eternal God. So if Jesus is the model Christian, then by definition, a Christian is a human being, but a human being that also has the divine life of the living God within them.

Being human, Jesus had his own will. But his own will never took precedent over what he knew to be the Father's will for him. Having the divine Spirit within him, he could perceive what the Father was leading him to do and say, and perfectly respond by obeying. Jesus was perfect in everything he did, everything he said, and in every circumstance he was in, whether it related to God, men, women, children, or angels.

We also learn from this story by seeing not only what Jesus did do, but also what he didn't do.

Lying around the Pool of Bethesda were perhaps hundreds of people that were sick, blind, lame, or withered. Why didn't Jesus just heal them all? As God, he certainly had the ability to do that. If he did, everyone in Jerusalem would have heard about such a miracle and he would have become famous overnight. Yet he only healed that one man? Why? Was it because he didn't have empathy and compassion for each one? He certainly did. The reason he only healed one person that day is because the Father showed Jesus that he was to go to the Pool of Bethesda and then showed him the one man he was to heal.

Following his Father's leading, Jesus stepped over and around dozens of pathetic and helpless bodies—all people with great need—but it was not until he came to this one man that he stopped. That was when Jesus heard the Father say, "This is the man I want you to heal today." So Jesus told the man to pick up his straw-filled mattress and walk. The man was instantly healed.

In today's context, if Jesus had healed the whole crowd, it would have been like someone going into a hospital and seeing every person healed, every bed vacated, every respirator and feeding tube left behind, and each patient walk out healed and made whole.

But that was not what the Father was leading Jesus to do. If Jesus had done that and healed everyone at the Pool of Bethesda that day, it would also have meant that he would have been disobedient to his Father by exercising his own will, and not the Father's. That act alone would have disqualified him from being our Savior. His Father only told him to heal that one man that day, so in perfect obedience, that is what he did.

I mentioned earlier that one of the themes in the Book of John is resting and abiding in Christ as a branch rests and abides in the vine (which we will explore more in depth later, particularly when we come to John chapter 15).

However, in the Old Testament, we see a curious thing. When the prophets Isaiah and Zechariah prophesied about the coming Messiah (Jesus), they referred to *him* as the branch, not the vine! Zechariah 6:12-13 (HCSB) says, "This is what the Lord of Hosts says: Here is a man whose name is Branch; He will branch out from His place and build the Lord's temple. Yes, he will build the Lord's temple; He will be clothed in splendor and will sit on His throne and rule."

As a man, Jesus laid aside his privileges and all the glory he had as God, emptied himself, took on the form of a lowly servant, and became our model for "branch living." As a branch, he humbled himself and became obedient to the vine-life of his Father living within him, even to the point of death—death on a cross. "For this reason God highly exalted Him and gave Him the name that is above every name, so that at the name of Jesus every knee will bow . . . and every tongue should confess that Jesus Christ is Lord, to the glory of God the Father" (Philippians 2:5-11 HCSB).

Now, as the exalted Lord of the universe, this perfect God-man Jesus has come to live in us through the Holy Spirit so that we could learn to live by his life, just as he lived by the life of his Father!

INCREASING REVELATION & MOUNTING ANTAGONISM FROM THE JEWS

CHAPTER 5

A man healed from thirty-eight years of suffering should have been cause for everyone in Jerusalem to rejoice. But for many Jews, the incident drove them over the edge, because Jesus healed the man on the Sabbath.

Jews celebrate the Sabbath beginning a few minutes before sunset on Friday evening until the appearance of three stars in the sky on Saturday night. The word "Sabbath" is a translation from the Hebrew noun *Shabbat*, which means "to cease," "to desist from something," and "to rest."

Its theological meaning stems from Genesis 2:2-3 where on the seventh day, after six days of creation, God rested. After the Bible's first mention of a day of rest, there was silence for more than 2,600 years—not another word on the subject. During that time, God chose Abraham and made a covenant (an agreement) with him, promising him that he would give him and his descendants a land to live in, that Abraham would become father of many nations, and that through him (and his descendants) all the nations of the earth would be blessed. Four hundred thirty years after that, God made a covenant of law with his people Israel through Moses, in which he gave them the Ten Commandments. It was not until then that keeping the Sabbath as a day of rest was enshrined as one of those commandments.

God instructed the people that for six days they should labor and do all their work, but the seventh day was to be a day of rest. At the heart of this observance, God had given them a day that would be dedicated completely to knowing and enjoying God by resting from their labors, affirming and acknowledging that God was their Creator and the sustainer of their lives.

Twice in John's Gospel the Pharisees accused Jesus of violating the Sabbath. The first time was when he healed the invalid man in chapter 5; later, in chapter 9, he also healed a man blind from birth. However, in Matthew's Gospel, Jesus said, "Do not think that I came to abolish the Law or the Prophets; I did not come to abolish but to fulfill" (Matthew 5:17). Jesus even pronounced a curse on anyone who broke even the least of the commandments and taught others to do so (Matthew 5:19). So why does he then break the law himself?

It's important to remember that God was the initiator of Sabbath-keeping when he gave the law of Moses. The original intent was that people would set aside one day a week to rest, enjoy God and their families, and remember that God was faithful and would provide for all their needs. But in Jesus' day, the Sabbath had become unrecognizably perverted. Religious leaders had piled burdensome traditions onto the law's original intent. For instance, one of those traditions (not found in the Bible) stated that if a fly crawled up a person's nose they couldn't do anything about it on the Sabbath because that would have been considered self-defense!

When Jesus formally began his public ministry in Nazareth (Luke 4:14-21), he stood in the local synagogue, picked up a scroll of Scripture, and read from Isaiah 61:1-2: "The Spirit of the Lord is upon Me, because he has appointed Me to preach the gospel to the poor. He has sent Me to proclaim release to the captives, and recovery of sight to the blind, to set free those who are oppressed, and to proclaim the favorable year of the Lord."

Jesus came to set his people free.

The observance of the Sabbath was and is central to Jewish life. But their view of the Sabbath had become petty and distorted. They were so pre-occupied with the trivial and the unimportant that they had totally lost sight of what God originally intended the Sabbath to be. Keeping the rules precisely, as they understood them, was more important than the good works that Jesus did and the wonderful healings he performed.

Both times in the Book of John when the Pharisees sparked Sabbath controversies with Jesus they were attempting to prove that Jesus was a law-breaker. If he was a law-breaker, he was a sinner. If he was a sinner, he could not be God. "Therefore some of the Pharisees were saying, 'This man is not from God, because He does not keep the Sabbath.' But others were saying, 'How can a man who is a sinner perform such signs?' And there was a division among them" (John 9:16).

Following the healing of the invalid man, Jesus said, "My Father has been working until now, and I have been working." When they heard him say, "My Father is working until now, and I myself am working," they sought all the more to kill him because not only was he breaking the Sabbath, but he also "was calling God His own Father, making Himself equal with God" (John 5:18).

Strictly speaking, if God stopped every kind of work he was involved with on the Sabbath, if he ceased all use of power, nature itself would devolve into chaos, sin would take over the world, the stars would fall from the sky, and the universe, as we know it, would cease to exist.

God works without ceasing 24/7, 365 days a year. He is continually at work upholding the universe and working on behalf of his people. Jesus Christ, as God incarnate, could decide the true meaning of the Sabbath because he created it. He demonstrated that the spirit of the law was to do good when the opportunity presented itself, even on the Sabbath. This is seen in Luke's Gospel when Jesus healed a man on the Sabbath whose right hand was paralyzed. One that occasion he asked the scribes and Pharisees if "It is lawful on the Sabbath to do what is good or to do what is evil, to save life or to destroy it?" (Luke 5:9) Then he immediately told the man to stretch out his hand and it was restored (v. 10).

At other times, when the Pharisees criticized Jesus for healing on the Sabbath, Jesus confounded them by saying that even they, sinful as they were, would not hesitate to pull a sheep out of a pit on the Sabbath. Because he came to seek and save his lost sheep, he would not allow a Sabbath day to stop him from working on their behalf (John 10:3, 27).

On another occasion, he questioned the Pharisees about why they were angry with him for healing a man on the Sabbath while they break the law of Moses themselves by circumcising a man on the Sabbath (John 7:23). The Jews could tolerate circumcising a baby boy on the Sabbath, but made it a capital offense for Jesus to heal a man on the Sabbath and make him completely whole.

Finally, on a day when Jesus and his disciples were walking through some grain fields on the Sabbath and his disciples were picking heads of grain and rubbing them together in their hands and eating them, the Pharisees challenged him once again, saying that this was not lawful (Luke 6:1-2). In response, he gave them an example from the Old Testament of David and his men, when they were hungry, entered the house of God and ate from the sacred bread. Then he closed with this, "The Son of Man is Lord of the Sabbath." (Luke 6:5)

Jesus personified the Sabbath rest. He was at rest and peace with God, yet he still worked. He offered mankind a spiritual rest from all their labors if they would come to him: "Come to Me, all who are weary and burdened, and I will give you rest" (Matthew 11:28 HCSB). He is available moment by moment. He is far superior to any Sabbath day, which was only observed one day per week.

As we cease striving to be holy by obeying the law, which is impossible to do anyway, and learn to rest in Jesus, his Spirit can then work in and through us, doing the things that are pleasing to God.

Let's pop back into the twenty-first century for a moment.

In the film *The Matrix*, Morpheus, Neo's mentor, drops some heavy truths on him when he describes the dream world Neo is living in, and the alternative reality Neo can choose to enter. Things like:

- "There's something wrong with this world, but you don't know what it is. The Matrix is here. It's all around us."
- "No one can tell you what the Matrix is. You have to see it for yourself."

- "All I'm offering you is the truth—nothing more."

After Neo takes the red pill, goes down the rabbit hole, and escapes the Matrix for the first time, he and Morpheus have this brief conversation:

> Morpheus: Welcome to the real world.
>
> Neo: Why do my eyes hurt?
>
> Morpheus: You've never used them before.

What does this have to do with Jesus and the Sabbath? John's Gospel gives us many wonderful revelations of Jesus Christ. But there is more to see, pertaining to the rest that Jesus offers, in other parts of the Bible as well. Another of our mentors, the Apostle Paul, who authored approximately 30 percent of the New Testament, weighs in on this in one of his letters to the believers living in Colossae:

> So why would you allow anyone to judge you because of
> what you eat or drink, or insist that you keep the feasts,
> observe new moon celebrations, or the Sabbath? All of
> these were but a prophetic shadow and the evidence of
> what would be fulfilled, for the body is now Christ!
> Colossians 2:16-17 TPT

I'm sure that you've had the experience of standing in the sun during the heat of the day and observing your shadow on the ground. Which is real? You? Or the shadow? You are the real deal! Your image on the ground is only a shadow.

Likewise, in these verses, Paul laser-focuses on the distinction between what is real, and what are only shadows. The really real deal is heavenly— from another realm, not what is seen. Jesus, who is in heaven, casts his shadow on the earth. Jesus is the substance, the body, and the reality of food, drink, feasts, *and* Sabbath days—all these shadows that we see here in our physical world on earth.

Welcome to the real world!

The Whole Bible Is About Jesus

CHAPTER 5

A final nugget we get to see in chapter 5 of the Book of John comes from a discussion Jesus had with the Jewish leaders regarding their Old Testament Scriptures (verses 39-46):

> You search the Scriptures because you think that in them
> you have eternal life; it is these that testify of Me; and you
> are unwilling to come to Me so that you may have life. . . .
> Do not think that I will accuse you before the Father; the
> one who accuses you is Moses, in whom you have set your
> hope. For if you believed Moses, you would believe Me,
> for he wrote about Me.

Moses was credited with writing the first five books of the Bible (which Jews also call the Torah): Genesis, Exodus, Leviticus, Numbers, and Deuteronomy. Let's take a step back for a moment and briefly review these five books, of which Jesus and the Jewish leaders would have been very familiar.

Genesis tells the story of creation, Adam and Eve and their descendants,

Noah and the flood, Abraham, and the beginnings of God working through his chosen people, Israel.

Exodus gives us the details on many things. It recounts how Moses was sent to free the Hebrews from slavery in Egypt, how they escaped to the wilderness by miraculously passing through the Red Sea, and how they received the law—the Ten Commandments, along with other laws and decrees telling the people the kind of life that love for God and their neighbor would require. Exodus also teaches us about the blueprints for the tabernacle that God gave to Moses and told him to construct. We also learn something about the priests that served the tabernacle and hear the story of the Israelite's pilgrimage through the desert en route to the Promised Land.

Leviticus describes the roles of the priests, the different offerings, the different feasts, moral laws, the blessings for keeping the laws, and the consequences for breaking them.

Numbers describes the raising up of an Israelite army and their preparation to take possession of the Promised Land.

Deuteronomy describes the good land that they inherited, with all its abundance and riches.

Though Jesus is not directly mentioned in the books of Moses, Jesus made the audacious statement that the books of Moses were not just history books, but they were written about him! We've already discussed many examples of how this is true in our coffee conversation so far.

In another passage from the Book of Luke, after his resurrection, Jesus appeared to two disciples heading out of Jerusalem on the road toward Emmaus. Luke wrote that during his encounter with these two disciples, this happened: "Then beginning with Moses and with all the prophets,

He explained to them the things concerning Himself in all the Scriptures" (Luke 24:27).

Shortly after that, Jesus appeared again, to a group of apostles and others who had been with him but who had not yet seen the resurrected Christ. During that appearance, Jesus said to them, "These are My words which I spoke to you while I was still with you, that all things which are written about Me in the Law of Moses and the Prophets and the Psalms must be fulfilled." Luke wrote that he then "opened their minds to understand the Scriptures" (Luke 24:44-45).

Through these verses we see that not only were the books of Moses written about Jesus, but so were all the books the prophets wrote, as well as all the Psalms and other poetry books contained in the thirty-nine books of the Old Testament!

To see Jesus in the Old Testament as well as in the New Testament Scriptures only comes by way of revelation. The Pharisees had head knowledge of their Scriptures. You might recall that they were required to memorize the entire Torah. They knew their Scriptures, but it was of no profit to them. They missed seeing Jesus in the words of Moses because they lacked revelation.

Are you beginning to see how central Jesus is in EVERYTHING?

There is so much to see about him. We could never take it in all at once. We've been given a lifetime to see more and more of him, and to become more like him.

If you are looking for one prayer to pray that will always line up with the heart of God, I would suggest this one for you:

"Lord Jesus, I want to know you better. Show me more of who you are!"

DAY 30

THE MIRACULOUS PICNIC

CHAPTER 6

Hungry this morning? How about some bread?

This morning we're going to look at two stories from John chapter 6. The first tells how Jesus miraculously fed about 10,000 people—at one time—with just five barley loaves and two fish! This was a picnic for the record books! In your Bible it says that Jesus fed 5,000. That's true. But that number did not include women and children.

The setting for this miracle was somewhere around the Sea of Galilee. John says that a large crowd was following Jesus because they had seen the miracles he performed. It was also around Passover time, when travelers were walking in large groups or caravans en route to Jerusalem to attend the feast. They heard Jesus was in the neighborhood, so many of them took a brief detour to catch a glimpse of this "prophet."

Jesus saw this crowd coming and he knew what he was going to do, so he turned to Philip and said something like this, just to test him: "Philip, these people are hungry, and there's no McDonalds anywhere in sight. What are we going to do to feed all these people?"

Philip probably scratched his head and didn't have a clue. He didn't see any stores either, but he was good at math so he did some quick mental calculations and responded something like, "Let's see. A day's wage is a denarii. A denarii might feed a man and his family of four or five for a whole day. That would mean 200 days' wages might feed about a thousand people for a whole day. But if we're just talking about a light snack, we may be able to stretch that to feed a few thousand. By my figuring, we're still coming up way short. Plus, we don't have that much money in the moneybag. So I don't think we're going to be able to pull this off!"

But, a young boy standing next to Philip had come prepared. He had brought his lunch along: five barley loaves and two fish. Jesus asked the lad if he would mind parting with his lunch. He gladly did. Jesus had the crowd sit down and then began breaking up the bread and the fish and passing it out to the crowd. Miraculously, the food did not run out. When everyone had finished eating, there was abundance for all, plus they had some left over.

The people were amazed! They thought, here's a prophet that can miraculously distribute free food. Let's make him king! We'll never have to worry about having something to eat again! But Jesus perceived what they were thinking and snuck away to be by himself.

The second story in chapter 6 involves the disciples leaving the scene that evening and getting into a large boat. They waited for Jesus, but he didn't show up, so they left on their own to head back to Capernaum. That had become the city where Jesus, for about a year and a half or so, had set up headquarters. They knew he would catch up with them.

About three or four miles into their journey on the sea, a strong storm with heavy winds came up out of nowhere. They were very afraid. Then they saw Jesus coming towards them, walking on the waves. They invited him into the boat, and immediately they arrived safely at their destination.

There are some great lessons we can learn from these stories! The first concerns the young lad. Here was a boy who offered what he had to Jesus, little though it was, and Jesus blessed it beyond anything he could have imagined. Whatever you possess—small or great—bring it to Jesus. Let him prove to you that he has the grace to bless and multiply what you offer to him, resulting in things you never thought possible!

It may be your home, which could be used for hospitality to bless others, or your financial resources. It doesn't matter if the gifts are little or large. The same goes with your time and your talents. Bring them to Jesus. Give them all to him so that he can fill you with joy, and you can be the one he uses to bless a hungry world in need.

More lessons are found in the story of the storm-tossed boat. This is a clear example of Jesus revealing his divine attributes by ruling over nature, calming the wind and the waves.

We can also learn something from Jesus' command to his disciples not to be afraid because of the storm.

"Don't be afraid," "Fear not," "Don't worry," or some derivative of that, is the most repeated command in the Bible.

What is it that you are afraid of or worried about? Is it what people think of you? Failing at something? Not having enough money? Losing a loved one? Death?

Jesus promised to never to leave you or forsake you. He is full of grace for those who are afraid. Peter instructs us to cast all our cares (worries, fears, anxieties) upon Christ, for he cares for us (1 Peter 5:7).

As soon as the disciples invited Jesus into their boat, the text says "immediately" they were brought to land. Inviting Jesus into your boat—your fearful, worrisome circumstances—will restore your peace and immediately bring you back to solid ground!

Outside of Jesus' time in the Garden of Gethsemane, hours before being crucified on a tree (we'll discuss that later when we come to it in the Gospel of John), do you ever see Jesus suffering from fear, anxiety, or worry? No. He was at peace because he constantly lived in the presence of his Father.

Remember, Jesus promised that he came to give you life—the same life that he lived by—and to give it to you in abundance. That's what you get in exchange for your fears!

Many people grow up having fear and anxiety as constant companions. But that is not how we were created to live. Trusting in and living in the presence of God there is no fear. Old habits die hard, and we are not going to get to that place all at once. But start having that conversation with Jesus today, whenever you become aware that rival thoughts are competing for your peace and trust in the Lord. The more you practice turning to the Lord and rejecting these old ways of thinking, the more it will become a way of life!

DAY 31

WHAT IS REAL BREAD?

CHAPTER 6

I want to start off this morning with a reminder. As you are going through the Book of John, or any book in the Bible for that matter, always pause before you begin, quiet your heart, and ask the Lord to reveal himself to you through the Scriptures. It takes God to reveal God.

Let's pick up where we left off in chapter 6. The crowd that had experienced the miraculous feeding followed Jesus to Capernaum, where they were probably hoping for more free food. But having gotten their attention by turning five barley loaves and two fish into a feast for a multitude, Jesus set the stage for a new revelation he wanted to give them.

Jesus began by telling the crowd that he had food to give away that was not physical but spiritual. One could not receive this food by working for it; faith was the only way to obtain it.

Then the crowd asked for another sign from him in order for them to believe. They recounted to him the story from Exodus 16 where God supernaturally provided bread from heaven (manna) to the Israelite pilgrims making their trek across the desert to the Promised Land. That group included "about six hundred thousand men on foot, besides their families" (Exodus 12:37 HCSB). If the Egyptians that joined the Israelites were counted as well as the women and children, that means the total number of people involved in the Exodus was somewhere around 2.5 to 3 million people. That's a lot of people that Jesus kept alive and fed for forty years in the wilderness!

But Jesus would not be controlled by giving the crowd the sign that they asked for. Instead, he responded by presenting them with a staggering new revelation that no one could have anticipated.

Using that story from Exodus, Jesus revealed that the bread that came from heaven that fed those three million souls in the wilderness was not real bread! It was only a picture, a shadow of real bread that neither they nor their ancestors understood. God is the one who gives the *real* or *true* heavenly bread. That bread is life-giving bread. Jesus shocked them by telling them that *he* was that bread!

Jesus said to them, "I am the bread of life; he who comes to Me will not hunger and he who believes in Me will never thirst" (John 6:35). To drive the point home, he repeated it again:

> I am the bread of life. Your fathers ate the manna in the wilderness, and they died. This is the bread which comes down out of heaven, so that one may eat of it and not die. *I am* the *living* bread that came down out of heaven; if anyone eats of this bread, he will live forever; and the bread also which I will give for the life of the world is My flesh.
>
> J O H N 6 : 4 8 - 5 1 , *emphasis mine*

Jesus presented himself to the Samaritan woman as water that was not from this world, water that was alive. Now he presented himself to this crowd as bread not of this world, but heavenly bread that was alive.

To illustrate: You've seen little children coloring in coloring books. If they're coloring a picture of a dog, in their minds, that picture *is* a dog. But then one day they see this excitable animal that moves and walks around, wags its tail, and licks their faces. It is then that they understand that *this* is a real dog! What they were coloring was just a picture of a dog.

Similarly, God created a world of "pictures," physical things—water, grains (bread), trees, seeds, fruit, stones, sun, moon, stars, etc.—that seem real to us, but they are not real in an ultimate sense. Using the movie *The Matrix* once more to explain this, Jesus gave them the red pill! But each individual still had to decide whether they were going to swallow it.

Jesus, the divine mastermind behind all creation, who was with God and was God at the beginning, knew what humans would need in order to survive in a physical universe; he knew this even before the physical heavens and earth were created. They would need water, they would need food, they would need sunlight, they would need air to breathe, etc. But Jesus lived in an alternate universe, a heavenly realm that was spiritual not physical. In that realm, God was the spiritual reality of the physical things he created. Jesus used this teaching to reveal this amazing truth so that every time we eat a piece of bread, every time we take a drink of water, every time we take a breath, we will have a daily reminder of who Jesus is and the spiritual reality that he wants us to be able to understand and to experience.

"As the living Father sent Me, and I live because of [or,

by] the Father, so he who eats Me, he also will live because
of [or, by] Me. This is the bread which came down out of
heaven; not as the fathers ate and died; he who eats this
bread will live forever"

JOHN 6:57, 58

Are you, by chance, eating a croissant, a cookie, a muffin, or a piece of
toast with your cup of coffee this morning? Look closely at it. What do
you see? Something real, or something else?

May God give you a revelation that will bring a smile! ☺

DAY 32

A HARD SAYING

CHAPTER 6

When Jesus started talking like this, saying that he was the bread that came from heaven, the Jews began to grumble. They were still seeing things on an earthly level. "Is this not Jesus, the son of Joseph, whose father and mother we know?"

Then Jesus dropped another truth bomb on them. "No one can come to Me unless the Father who sent Me draws him; and I will raise him up on the last day" (John 6:44). He also said, "This is the will of Him who sent Me, that of all that He has given Me, I lose nothing, but raise it up on the last day" (John 6:39).

This should give you great comfort. God is not one who would give something, and then take it back. You are the Father's gift to Jesus! And once Jesus receives a gift from the Father (all those who come to him), he will not cast that gift away (John 6:37).

You'll notice how many times throughout this passage Jesus says that he will give eternal life to those who believe. In one sense he was saying that those who believe would live forever, but in another sense, he was telling them about the quality of the life that he had to offer—that it was transcendent, eternal in nature, the *zoe* life that he lived by himself.

Then Jesus gave them a more difficult pill to swallow. He said, "The bread also which I will give for the life of the world is My flesh" (John 6:51). That really riled the Jews up and they began to argue among themselves, saying, "How can this man give us *His* flesh to eat?"

Jesus did not soothe them when he added, "Truly, truly I say to you, unless you eat the flesh of the Son of Man and drink His blood, you have no life in yourselves. . . . For My flesh is true food, and My blood is true drink" (John 6:53, 55).

Verse 60 says, "Therefore many of His disciples, when they heard this said, 'This is a difficult statement; who can listen to this?'" Even his loyal followers—the twelve—had difficulty swallowing this one.

Let me translate for you what they were thinking: "Are we talking cannibalism here? Some Satanic blood-drinking ceremony? This guy has got to be crazy! We can't listen to this."

But now that he had their attention, Jesus made his main point: "It is the Spirit who gives life; the flesh profits nothing; the words that I have spoken to you are spirit and are life."

Jesus wasn't talking about literally eating his flesh or drinking his blood. That is pretty disgusting and wouldn't profit anybody anything—in fact, it would make them vomit. He was talking about eating and drinking the Spirit of life; the words he was speaking to them were spirit and were life.

But still, many did not understand. They withdrew and stopped following him.

Jesus then turned to the twelve and said to them, "You do not want to go away also, do you?"

Peter answered him, "Lord, to whom shall we go? You have words of eternal life. We have believed and have come to know that You are the Holy One of God" (John 6:68-69).

This was another "red pill" moment. Like Peter, once you have seen and understood the reality of who Jesus is, you will never be the same and never be satisfied with anything else again.

Jesus & the Feast of Booths (Tabernacles)

CHAPTER 7

The seventh and eighth chapters of John are connected. They both describe events that took place within the same short span of time.

Chapter 7 begins with Jesus in Galilee, unwilling to go to Judea because he knew the Jews there wanted to kill him.

In Jesus' time, the land we know as Israel today was divided into three provinces—Galilee in the north, Judea in the south, where Jerusalem was located, and Samaria in between.

It took about five or six days to walk from Galilee to Jerusalem, depending on the direction one took. The shortcut was through Samaria, but most devout Jews took a longer route due to their racial distain for Samaritans.

Judeans looked down on Galileans. They considered the Galileans a crude country crowd, while the Judeans prided themselves on being sophisticated city folk. Galileans spoke a dialect that was not as upscale as what was spoken in Judea, and they were often the butt of jokes. Galileans in Jerusalem probably felt the same way a West Virginian farmer feels on the crowded streets of Manhattan.

It was now the year before Jesus' crucifixion. Another one of the annual feasts—the Feast of Booths, which took place at the end of harvest season—had once again arrived, and all Jewish males were required to attend. The men came from all around Judea and different nations throughout the Roman Empire, while most women were left behind to care for children, their animals, their crops, and their households.

At this time, even Jesus' own brothers (really half-brothers) still did not believe Jesus' true identity and treated him with some distain and ridicule. Mockingly, they suggested that if he really were the Messiah, Jerusalem was the place to reveal it, and this Feast of Booths would be the time to do it. Jesus responded by telling them that his time had not yet come.

His brothers left for the feast. Jesus stayed behind in Galilee but later went secretly, by himself, and arrived halfway through the celebration. This was a fearless move on Jesus' part because he knew the intentions of the Jewish leaders to catch and kill him.

To celebrate this weeklong autumn festival, people made temporary shelters, or booths, from palm and willow branches. These booths filled Jerusalem's streets and squares, as well as dotted the fields, gardens, vineyards, orchards, hills, and housetops. They became peoples' homes for a week, where they lived, ate, slept, prayed, meditated, and rested. This was to remind them of the temporary shelters their ancestors had used during their time of wandering in the desert.

On the last day of this feast all attention focused on a final ritual performed by a priest. The priest would go out from the Temple with a golden pitcher to draw water from the Pool of Siloam. The sweet waters of the Gihon Spring, over which the Temple was built, fed this pool.

After fetching the water, the priest reentered the Temple to the sound of blasting trumpets. A second priest, carrying a pitcher of wine, would join him. Together, they ascended the sloping ramp to the altar (on which sacrifices were made), and emptied the contents of the pitchers on the altar as a drink offering to the Lord. The priest then read aloud a portion of Scripture from Isaiah 12: "Therefore you will joyously draw water from the springs of salvation. . . . Cry aloud and shout, O inhabitant of Zion, for great in your midst is the Holy One of Israel." (Zion was one of the mountains in the vicinity of Jerusalem upon which the City of David was built. It later became synonymous with Jerusalem itself.)

The water the priest poured out served as a reminder of when Moses struck a rock in the wilderness that produced water for the Israelites. It also had a future application. It was done in anticipation of God sending rain for the coming harvest, as well as a reminder of another prophecy from both Ezekiel and Zechariah. These prophecies foretold of a day when waters would flow out from the Temple and Jerusalem, becoming waters of life and healing. Ezekiel wrote, ". . . every living creature which swarms in every place where the river goes, will live," and "By the river on its bank . . . will grow all kinds of trees for food . . . and their fruit will be for food and their leaves for healing" (Ezekiel 47:9, 12).

During this final ritual at the peak of the festival, with thousands in attendance, music playing, psalms (songs) being sung, and people joyfully waving their palm and willow branches in the air—something unimaginable happened. During a brief moment of silence after the trumpets had sounded, Jesus bellowed out from the crowd in a voice that could be heard by all, "If anyone is thirsty, let him come to Me and drink! He who believes in Me, as the Scripture said, from his innermost being will flow rivers of living water" (John 7: 37-38).

The Holy One of Israel *was* in their midst!

That must have been a real showstopper!

John immediately interpreted this event in the next verse: "But this He spoke of the Spirit, whom those who believed in Him were to receive; for the Spirit was not yet given, because Jesus was not yet glorified" (verse 39).

Much more to say on this, but I'll have to leave you hanging until tomorrow!

JESUS, THE REALITY
OF THE FEASTS

CHAPTER 7

Just like the Passover, the Feast of Booths spoken of in the Old Testament was another festival fulfilled in the person of Jesus. Not only was he the real Lamb who would take away the sin of the world (Passover), but he was also the fulfillment of the drink offering poured out by the priests. As the life-giving Spirit, he would be the river that would bring healing and life everywhere he flowed.

He was also the reality behind the picture of the booths where the people lived, ate, slept, and prayed. In a message the Apostle Paul delivered to a group of Gentiles in Athens, Greece, he proclaimed to them, "For in Him [God] we live and move and exist" (Acts 17:28).

The word "Christian" occurs only three times in the Bible. But expressions like "in Christ," "in the Lord," and "in him" occur 164 times in Paul's letters alone.

Jesus is not only in us, but we are "in him," represented by the people living in these booths. This is a subject John will continue to develop later in the book.

Everyone in the crowd was stunned. But they were divided on what to make of his words. Some were saying, "This is the Christ!" Others at least recognized what he said as being prophetic. Still others were perplexed and wondered who Jesus was. Nothing like this had ever happened before. Even the temple guards, who were supposed to keep order at these celebrations, were so shocked and spellbound that they did not know what to do. No one dared lay a hand on him.

There was some dispute among the Jews over whether or not Jesus could be the Christ. They appeared confused over where he had come from. They knew, from Old Testament prophesies, that the Messiah would come from the descendants of David and the city of Bethlehem, but they also knew that Jesus was from Galilee. So how then could Jesus be the Messiah? What the crowd didn't realize was that Jesus had indeed been born in Bethlehem. Some thirty-two years prior, a census was taken of all the Roman Empire. Jesus' parents, Joseph and Mary, lived in Nazareth, in the Galilee region. Joseph was a descendant from the family of David. He and his pregnant wife, Mary, had to travel to Bethlehem to register for the census. It was there that Jesus was born. A few years later the family returned to Nazareth, where Jesus grew up and was raised. (You can read about this in Luke chapter 2.)

There's much more to say about this festival, but next John throws in a story about a woman brought to Jesus who was caught in adultery.. Tomorrow we'll look at what happened with this woman, and then we'll return to some more amazing symbolism concerning this feast.

Jesus & the Woman Caught in Adultery

CHAPTER 8

The next story in chapter 8 of John's Gospel is the story of an adulterous woman. This event took place in the Temple, the very next morning after Jesus proclaimed to the crowd that he was the living water for which they were hoping and praying.

Many readers, after reading this story of the adulterous woman, are left wondering about the man who was caught in the illicit sex act with her. Why was he not dragged before Jesus to be stoned as well? That answer we will never know.

The simple facts of the story go like this:

1. This woman had been caught in adultery.
2. The Jews thought she should be stoned because that was the punishment prescribed in the law for anyone committing such an act.
3. Jesus told her accusers: "The one without sin among you should be the first to throw a stone at her." (John 8:7)

4. Each of the woman's accusers, beginning with the oldest, then dropped their stones and walked away because they were convicted that they were sinners also.
5. After telling the woman that he did not condemn her, he sent her on her way.
6. The dialogue then resumed with these judgmental men, and Jesus gave them another potent dose of revelatory truth.
7. By the end of chapter 8 they had picked up their stones again, but this time they wanted to stone Jesus.
8. Jesus hid himself from them and went out of the Temple.

Between the basic facts, other details emerge that provide rich context to the story.

While her accusers were questioning Jesus regarding his interpretation of the law requiring that the woman be stoned, John writes that, "Jesus stooped down and started writing on the ground with His finger" (John 8:6 HCSB).

What did he write on the ground? We don't know, really. But nothing Jesus ever did was by accident. There must have been some explanation.

Jeremiah chapter 17, verse 13 says, "Lord, the hope of Israel, all who abandon You will be put to shame. All who turn away from Me will be written in the dirt, for they have abandoned the Lord, the fountain of living water." (HCSB)

The night before, Jesus claimed to be the living water. Could it be that Jesus took this opportunity to fulfill this Scripture from Jeremiah relating to those who had rejected him as the living water?

Although the Scripture is silent on what Jesus wrote, it's possible that

Jesus used his finger to write this verse from Jeremiah in the dust.

Jesus then straightened up and said to them, "The one without sin among you should be the first to throw a stone at her." (HCSB) Then he stooped down again and began writing on the ground once more. What could he have written this time?

Again, the Scripture is silent on what he wrote. But could it be that he began writing each of their names in the dust, just as the passage from Jeremiah says the Lord, the hope of all Israel, would do?

Regardless, when they heard what Jesus said and saw what he had written in the sand, they were stunned and convicted. They dropped their stones and began to walk away.

The woman must have felt so embarrassed, shame-filled, and condemned. She was probably cowering and trembling, awaiting a sentence from Jesus that would confirm her accusers' charges. But instead, when she looked up at Jesus with tear-filled eyes, she was met with the totally unexpected tenderness and unsurpassing grace of a loving Savior. Grace for those who are caught in their sins and deserve to die! Through Jesus' love she received a pardon and walked away free.

As if the drama and excitement of the past twenty-four hours were not enough, Jesus was not finished. He divulged even more revelatory information to the woman's accusers, as well as to others in the Temple, where he was teaching. The passage continues, "Then Jesus again spoke to them, saying, 'I am the Light of the world; he who follows Me will not walk in darkness, but will have the Light of life'" (John 8:12).

More great stuff on this tomorrow!

JESUS, THE LIGHT
OF THE WORLD

CHAPTER 8

Everything we really need to know concerning spiritual things is in the Bible. Yet, historical information provided by other sources can be helpful in filling out an already bright and vibrant picture with more subtle details.

Supplementary material about the Feast of Booths comes from other rabbinical writings outside the Bible—specifically from the Talmud. The Talmud is the written version of what was called the Traditions of the Elders that existed in oral form in Jesus' day.

According to Jewish scholars, the Hebrew Bible (our Old Testament) contains a total of 613 laws—ten of which were spoken orally by God on Mt. Sinai, which we know as the Ten Commandments. The others are found in the writings of Moses.

The Traditions of the Elders sought to expand upon Biblical texts and explain them more precisely. For instance, concerning the Feast of Booths, the law of Moses instructed people to make booths or shelters to live in. But it didn't say how big a booth was to be, how many doors it was to have, if it should have windows (air conditioning!), or how it was to be constructed. The extra-Biblical body of oral tradition originated in questions like these.

Following the destruction of Jerusalem in 70 A.D., when the Jewish people were scattered throughout the world, Jewish scholars and rabbis feared that the people would forget these traditions, so sometime in the second century they began to put them into writing in a book called the Mishnah. Over the next few centuries this work was expanded, resulting in a second book called the Germana. When combined, these two books comprise what is referred to today as the Talmud.

The entire Talmud embodies the contribution of hundreds of Jewish rabbis, consists of sixty-three volumes, and in standard print is over 6,200 pages long. Though the Talmud has become the primary source for Jewish interpretation of the Scriptures, Jesus had many heated and rigorous disputes with the Pharisees of his day over these oral traditions. These traditions had become so important, and the Pharisees clung to them so fiercely, that they even came to be elevated to the same level of inspiration as the Scriptures themselves.

That said, the Talmud can still teach us some things about this historical celebration—the Feast of Booths—that are helpful in giving us a rich backdrop for Jesus' teaching that he is the Light of the world.

This feast featured *two* major symbols, water *and* light. I've already commented on the water. The light was represented by the candela-bra-lighting ceremony. Within the Temple, in the court of the women where the treasury was located, four great candelabras were erected for this special occasion.

Young men climbed up on several ladders that were leaned against these tall candelabras, filled them with oil, and lit them with a torch. The light from these blazing lamps lit up not only the whole Temple, but all of Jerusalem as well. They served as a reminder of the pillar of fire that had led the people through the desert by night to the Promised Land. It is with this backdrop that Jesus said, "I am the Light of the world!"

What was he announcing here? Jesus was telling the people (and us) that he was the *real* light who would take us to the *real* Promised Land!

God had given the land of Canaan to the Jews. It was to be their inheritance. It was a good land, flowing with milk and honey, wheat and oil, figs and vines, rich minerals, rivers, mountains, and valleys—all the people would ever need.

But that Promised Land was only a picture. Our inheritance is far greater. Our inheritance is found in that other realm. Our inheritance is God himself, in the person of Jesus!

This celebration in Jerusalem was never intended to be for the Jews only. Jesus also fulfilled another prophesy by Isaiah that the Messiah of Israel would be a light to all the nations of the world (Isaiah 42:6, 49:6).

Jesus is so rich! He is the river of life, our light, and our inheritance. But there is more.

From this point onward, through the end of the chapter 8, John will take us to the summit to see the highest revelation in the Bible of who Jesus was, coming from Jesus' own lips.

Stay tuned. Don't miss tomorrow!

JESUS, THE "I AM"

CHAPTER 8

In the midst of chapter 8, an ongoing exchange took place between Jesus, the antagonistic scribes and Pharisees who had brought the adulterous woman to him, and another group of Jews who were at the scene.

Following Jesus' announcement that he was the Light of the world, the scribes and Pharisees asserted that his testimony was not true. Jesus rebuffed them and said that it *was* true, and that they didn't know where he had come from (the Father) or where he was going (back to the Father). They had based their understanding solely on an earthly, fleshly orientation, so they thought he was referring to his earthly stepfather, Joseph, and his hometown in Galilee.

It was then that Jesus began talking to them about his true Father.

Not one time anywhere in the Hebrew Scriptures had any individual ever referred to God as his own father. But Jesus told them that it was his Father—God—who had sent him, and it was the Father who testified concerning him. Jesus only spoke things he heard from his Father, he only did things that were pleasing to the Father, and his Father was with him.

Those antagonistic Jews and Pharisees, on the other hand, did not know his Father.

Jesus then had a brief, sidebar conversation with another group of Jews that were present and had believed in him that day. What he said to them is often quoted (mostly out of context, unfortunately): "You will know the truth and the truth will make you free" (John 8:32).

Those antagonistic Jews then chimed in and said, "We are Abraham's descendants and have never been enslaved to anyone; how is it that You say, 'You will become free.'"

They were obviously willfully uninformed because many nations had enslaved the Jews in the past—the Egyptians, Assyrians, Babylonians, and now the Romans. But facts didn't matter. Regardless, they were thinking of freedom in terms of earthly things and specifically, political freedom.

Jesus continued speaking to them from his heavenly perspective. From heaven's perspective, they were slaves not to other nations but to sin. "Truly, truly, everyone who commits sin is a slave to sin," Jesus said (v. 34). "So if the Son makes you free, you shall be free indeed" (v. 36).

Only Jesus had the power and the authority to set a person free from sin, as he had demonstrated with the adulterous woman.

Jesus then confronted the Jews' claims to be descendants of Abraham and their assertion that Abraham was their father. He told them they were not and that this was not true—another big slap in their faces! Finally, they said to him, "We have one father, God."

Jesus responded,

> If God were your father, you would love Me, for I
> proceeded forth and have come from God. . . . You are of
> your father the devil, and you want to do the desires of
> your father. He was a murderer from the beginning and
> does not stand in the truth because there is no truth in
> him . . . for he is a liar, and the father of lies.
>
> J O H N 8 : 4 2 - 4 4

Excuse me???

Abraham is not our father, God is not our father, but our father is the devil???

No doubt, this made them very angry. But what he was about to reveal went far beyond making them angry. It made them furious. I mean vein-popping, heart-attack-producing type of furious. Furious enough for them to want to stone him to death.

Twice before in this dialogue Jesus made statements that they must not have picked up on or that had not "clicked" with them yet. The first was in verse 24: "Therefore I said to you that you will die in your sins; for unless you believe that I am *He,* you will die in your sins." The second was in verse 28: "When you lift up the Son of Man, then you will know that I am *He,* and I do nothing on my own initiative, but I speak these things as the Father taught me."

In most translations of the Bible, the translators did us a great disservice with both verses quoted in the above paragraph. You'll notice that the word "*He*" is in italics. That means that it does not appear in the original language, Greek, but is implied. The translators inserted *He* in an attempt to assist us in our understanding. What Jesus meant to say, and the way these verses should actually read is something like this: "Unless you believe that 'I AM,' you will die in your sins; and when the Son of Man is lifted up [on the cross], then you will know that 'I AM.'"

"I AM"—appears once more in the closing dialogue of the chapter. The Jews said that surely Jesus was not greater than Abraham, and Jesus responded by saying, "Abraham rejoiced to see My day, and he saw and was glad."

They shot back, "You are not yet fifty years old, and have You seen Abraham?"

Jesus did not hold back. He pulled back the curtain and gave them the highest revelation of himself that he would ever utter: "Truly, truly, I say to you, before Abraham was born, I AM." (John 8:58)

Hearing this for a third time, they finally realized what he meant!

In the Book of Exodus, chapter 3, God appeared to Moses in a burning tumbleweed in the hot desert and commissioned him to return to Egypt to set God's people free. Moses inquired of God, "What is your name? Who shall I say has sent me?" Then "God said to Moses, 'I AM WHO I AM;' and He said, 'Thus you shall say to the sons of Israel, "I AM has sent me to you"'" (Exodus 3:14).

Point blank, Jesus told these Jews that not only did he exist before Abraham, but he was the eternal one, the I AM. The very God who had appeared to Moses in the burning bush was now standing there in the flesh staring them in the face.

The Jews believed that there was only one God in the Old Testament, Jehovah. This was true. But now Jesus was as self-revealing to them as he could possibly be. In essence, what he said to them was this: Jehovah God, the God from your own sacred book who you have read about and say you worship, is standing before you this very minute. I am HE!

They came apart. They totally lost it. They could not receive this, so they picked up stones to stone him to death. Jesus' crime: blasphemy, for he had declared himself to be God.

To reject Jesus is a serious matter. To reject Jesus is to reject God, and by rejecting God, a person will die in their sins (John 8:24).

The resurrection was proof that Jesus was God (the I AM)—John 8:28.

Jews then and now, who say that they believe in the God of the Old Testament, do not really believe in the one and only living God, because if they did, they would believe also in Jesus.

John's Gospel unfolds a progressive revelation of who Jesus is. In John 4:26 he said, "I am the Messiah;" in John 6:36 he said, "I am the Bread of Life;" in John 8:12 he said, "I am the Light of the world." Now in John 8, verses 24, 28, and 58, he said, "I am the I AM."

Jesus Christ is the eternal God, and as we shall continue to see, his "I am" statements do not end here. He is not only the eternal one; he is the "I AM" of the present, ready to be for us whatever it is that we need!

Amazing, amazing!

JESUS, & THE HEALING OF THE BLIND BEGGAR

CHAPTER 9

As we begin chapter 9 of John, nearly two months had passed since Jesus caused all the commotion at the Feast of Booths. It was now the beginning of winter—late November to early December. Jesus was in Jerusalem once again for another feast, the Feast of Dedication.

This feast is not mentioned anywhere in the Old Testament because it originated during the period of about 400 years between when the last of the Old Testament books (Malachi) was written and when Jesus was born. It commemorated the rededication of the Jewish temple after it had been desecrated and partially destroyed by an invading Syrian army. You've probably heard of it by another name. It's synonymous with what the Jews today celebrate as Hanukkah.

Jewish people also refer to Hanukkah as the Festival of Lights. They celebrate it by lighting a candlestick called a menorah. The original menorah was made of gold, had seven branches, and was part of the furnishings in the wilderness tabernacle and in the Temple in Jerusalem. The Talmud forbids that a seven-branch menorah be used outside the Temple. That's why today, you will see Jews use an eight- or nine-branched menorah in their homes or synagogues for their Hanukkah celebration.

Chapters 8, 9, and 10 of the Book of John actually flow together. In chapter 8, Jesus said that he was the Light of the world and declared himself to be the "I AM"—the living God. In this chapter, chapter 9, Jesus healed a man who was blind from birth. This man became the prime illustration, the poster child, for what Jesus had taught at the last feast. Jesus was the Light of the world, bringing light and sight to those who were born in darkness. And this proved the fact that he was the "I AM," because only God could heal a man that was born blind. Chapter 10 builds on the story of this blind man that Jesus healed.

It is not insignificant, then, that Jesus chose the Festival of Lights to demonstrate concretely that he is a greater light—the reality of Light—who gives light to the world.

Chapter 9 begins with this: "As He passed by, He saw a man blind from birth."

This man was *born* blind. Other instances in the gospels that tell of Jesus healing the blind involved people who had seen before. Before I get too far, let me say this: we are all like that man. Though we may physically see, we were all born spiritually blind. As you read the story of this man, think of yourself in his place.

In the gospel narratives, Jesus healed blind people in a number of ways, so he is not limited in the way he performs miracles. But the way Jesus healed this man seems very, very strange. First, Jesus spat on the ground and made clay of the spittle. He placed the mud on the man's eyes. Then he sent him away to wash in the Pool of Siloam, and the man came back seeing.

What a prescription for healing blindness!

But was there more to it than we read on the surface? Was Jesus not only healing a blind man, but also sending a message to the Jews?

You see, in the Jewish oral traditions there was a law. A strange law, for sure. Where it originated, we don't know, but we can read about it in the fine print in that long book of 6,200 pages called the Talmud, where it was codified in writing. The Talmud states, "To heal a blind man on the Sabbath . . . it is . . . prohibited to make mud with spittle and smear it on his eyes" (Shabbat 108:2, if you want to be specific!).

Jesus not only healed the blind man on the Sabbath, which was against Jewish law, but he purposely used mud with spittle in direct defiance to some of their moronic traditions!

Tell me that Jesus didn't go out of his way to make a point that he was totally opposed to useless religion. He wanted people to know *him*!

The neighbors (apparently), and some of those who had previously seen him as a beggar, brought the formerly blind man to the Pharisees to explain to them how he was healed. Sadly, the Pharisees didn't care a whit about the man or rejoice with him at his healing. They just wanted to nail Jesus. "This man [Jesus] is not from God, because He does not keep the Sabbath," the Pharisees said to each other (John 9:16). But they did ask the healed man who he thought Jesus was. The man said, "He is a prophet."

Well, they'd had enough of him, so they called the man's parents in to question *them*. The parents confirmed that this was their son and that he was born blind. But they were reluctant to say who had healed him, because they were afraid. They knew that the Jewish leaders had already agreed that if anyone confessed Jesus to be the Messiah, they would be thrown out of the synagogue. So they passed the buck, and told the Pharisees that if they wanted to know more about this, they'd have to ask their son because he was mature enough to answer them directly.

The Pharisees then called the formerly blind beggar back in and began grilling him again. They were still hung up on Jesus being a sinner because he healed the man on a Sabbath day.

The man responded, "Whether He is a sinner, I do not know; one thing I do know, that though I was blind, now I see. . . . I told you already [how he opened my eyes] and you did not listen; why do you want to hear it again? You do not want to become His disciples too, do you?" (John 9:25-27).

In short order, the man had grown from believing that Jesus was a prophet and a healer, to thinking of himself as Jesus' disciple. It is amazing to watch how the more this man talked about Jesus, the stronger his faith became.

The Pharisees were insulted. Yet they continued to reveal their own blindness as they reviled and debated with the man. "You are His disciple, but we are disciples of Moses. We know that God has spoken to Moses, but as for this man, we do not know where He is from" (John 9:28-29).

In a matter of seconds, this man's stature skyrocketed once again. He went from being a blind man, to a disciple, and now to a bold prophet himself—one they could not compete with. His faith became strong when it was challenged and tested.

John wrote,

The man answered and said to them, "Well, here is an
amazing thing, that you do not know where He is from,
and yet He opened my eyes. We know that God does
not hear sinners; but if anyone is God-fearing and does
his will, he hears him. Since the beginning of time it has
never been heard that anyone opened the eyes of a person
born blind. If this man were not from God, He could do
nothing."

JOHN 9:30-33

The implications of what this man said to the Pharisees were staggering.
They didn't know where Jesus had come from, but this man did. The
Pharisees thought Jesus was a sinner, but they were the sinners because
God was not listening to them. They were not God-fearing or doing the
will of God—but the beggar was.

Exasperated, the Pharisees abruptly ended the conversation and did to
the beggar what his parents had feared. They branded him an unbeliever
and ostracized him; then they threw him out of the synagogue.

The next verses are very tender.

Jesus heard that they had put the man out, and finding him, he said, "Do
you believe in the Son of Man?"

The beggar answered, "Who is He, Lord, that I may believe in Him?"

Jesus said to him, "You have both seen Him, and He is the one who is
talking with you."

And the beggar said, "Lord, I believe." And he worshipped Him.

This man—who had already come a long way—had now come even

further. He had acknowledged Jesus as a prophet, as a healer, as one sent from God, and now he was calling him "Lord" and becoming a worshipper.

Isn't this the path we, too, have been called to walk—to know Jesus as Lord and worship him? But do you realize that to do this, there is a price to pay? It involves a radical departure from false, blinding, legalistic, man-made religion into a relationship with Jesus alone. It might involve ostracism. It might even involve suffering. And in extreme cases, such as in the Muslim world today, it may even involve death.

Is this a price you are willing to pay?

JESUS, THE GOOD SHEPHERD

CHAPTER 9

Chapter 9 and the story of the blind beggar ends with this: "If you [Pharisees] were blind," Jesus told them, "you would have no sin; but since you say, 'We see,' your sin remains.'"

Chapter 10 begins with a metaphor of a different kind: "Truly, truly, I say to you, he who does not enter by the door into the fold of the sheep, but climbs up some other way, he is a thief and a robber. But he who enters by the door is a shepherd of the sheep. To him the doorkeeper opens, and the sheep hear his voice, and he calls his own sheep by name and leads them out."

When the books of the Bible were originally written, there were no such things as chapters or verses. Each book (or scroll) was one continuous document. Chapter divisions first appeared in the thirteenth century. Verses were added in the sixteenth century. This was done for convenience to make it easier to find certain passages. But they were also arbitrary (not divinely inspired), and sometimes they interfere with the flow of a passage, as happens in this case. Chapter 10 does not introduce us to a new story with a new setting. It was a continuation of what Jesus was saying to the Pharisees, indicating to them that they were not the true shepherds of God's sheep, but were false shepherds—thieves and robbers.

There are many characters and objects mentioned in this allegory: a shepherd, sheep, a doorkeeper, a stranger, thieves and robbers, a hired hand, a sheepfold, a door, and a pasture. To sort all this out, I'm going to make it as simple as possible, walking through one item at a time.

Let's start with the sheep. Sheep are helplessly stupid animals. They don't have claws; they don't have fangs; they don't have sharp quills; they have no natural ability to protect themselves. They have no sense of direction and are prone to wander. As the prophet Isaiah wrote, "We are all like sheep that go astray and turn to our own way" (Isaiah 53:6). What a wonderful animal God chose to represent us! Our only hope is to have a good shepherd who will care for us and protect us.

What is a sheepfold? As the name implies, a sheepfold is a pen where the sheep stay at night when it is dark, when there is danger close by, or when there's a storm. In Jesus' day, the shepherds usually constructed a pen in a field by making walls out of rocks, leaving just one small entrance, through which the sheep were let in and out. The pen had a security system—not like the electronic ones today, but something much more primitive. The shepherd simply slept in front of the entrance way so that no sheep could get out, and no hungry animals could get in. He was the door.

In this allegory, Jesus said that he was both the shepherd and the door. During the day, the shepherd would lead the sheep from pasture to pasture to eat and to the nearest stream or watering hole where they could drink. In the same way, Jesus shepherds us, his flock, leading us away from danger and toward safe and fruitful territory where we can eat and drink and be satisfied.

God established the "sheepfold" of Judaism in the Old Testament. He put all of his people in the protective custody of this fold, giving them laws and rules to protect them so they wouldn't kill each other, waiting for the day that Jesus would come.

The thieves, the robbers, the strangers, and the hired hands—those who were just in it for the money—these were the Pharisees and religious leaders. They were the false shepherds. They claimed to be the protectors of the sheep, but were really not. They were supposed to lovingly care for the sheep, but if the blind man was any example, they certainly did not. They could only kill, steal, and destroy. Only Jesus could give life.

True shepherds named their sheep. When the sheep were in the pen, the shepherd would call their names, the sheep would recognize the shepherd's voice, and they would go out to feed in the green pastures. A true shepherd would also go to war with lions, bears, and other predators and be willing to fight tooth and nail, even to the death, to protect his sheep.

In the Old Testament, God had the same problem with the Jewish religious leaders more than 600 years earlier. Ezekiel chapter 34 speaks about the false and selfish shepherds of Israel who had abandoned God's sheep. God had to step in. In this passage he said:

- I will deliver my flock from the false shepherds.
- I will search for my sheep and seek them out.
- I will care for my sheep. I will gather them and feed them.
- I will feed them in good pasture.
- I will feed my flock and I will lead them to rest.
- I will bind up the broken and strengthen the sick.
- I will deliver my flock and they shall no longer be a prey.
- We are his sheep; the sheep of his pasture.

Another good "shepherd passage" from the Old Testament is the Shepherd's Psalm, Psalm 23. (A Psalm is a song. This is one David wrote):

> The L O R D is my shepherd,
> I shall not want.
> He makes me lie down in green pastures;
> He leads me beside quiet waters.
> He restores my soul;
> He guides me in the paths of righteousness
> For His name's sake.
> Even though I walk through
>   the valley of the shadow of death,
> I fear no evil, for You are with me;
> Your rod and Your staff, they comfort me.
> You prepare a table before me in the presence of my
>   enemies;
> You have anointed my head with oil;
> My cup overflows.
> Surely goodness and lovingkindness
> will follow me all the days of my life,
> And I will dwell in the house of the Lord forever.

Now, let's go back and see how the Great Shepherd, Jesus, dealt with one of his sheep, the formerly blind man.

This formerly blind man was a sheep locked inside the pen of Judaism. Chapter 9 says that the Pharisees expelled him from the synagogue. They kicked him out. But in chapter 10, verse 2, Jesus said that his sheep hear his voice, he calls his own sheep by name, and *he leads them out*. It may have looked like the man was kicked out, but it was really Jesus who led him out. Jesus had a better pasture than Judaism for this man to feed in.

Jesus also said that he had other sheep, not of this pen. These sheep would hear his voice and he would bring them out of their pens as well. These were non-Jewish people—the Gentiles—who would hear his voice and respond to his call once the Spirit came and the gospel spread to the whole world. These two groups of sheep—believing Jews and believing Gentiles—would become one flock (the Church), with one shepherd.

But what really got to the Pharisees was when Jesus said, "I am the Good Shepherd."

Where the Shepherd Psalm said, "The LORD [Jehovah] is my shepherd," Jesus was claiming to be *that* shepherd! In verse 30, Jesus even told them once again that he and the Father were one. But they still could not hear his voice.

Once again they picked up stones to stone him. Blasphemy again. (There must have been stones everywhere. How many times before had they picked up stones to stone him?) But they couldn't quite pull the trigger, because his hour had not yet come.

Jesus did not fit in Judaism. He did not fit in a man-made religious system. He didn't go to their schools. He didn't have their theology. He was different. He didn't conform to their traditions. He was not legalistic or self-righteous, but full of grace, compassion, and mercy.

When Jesus was on this earth, he was rejected by the religious system. When they found he would not conform, they tried to destroy him. But the religious system was also something he rejected.

This is the story of Jesus and the blind beggar: the Good Shepherd, and one of his precious sheep. There are many spiritual discoveries and applications in this story. But one thing is for sure: just like it had for that blind beggar, it could very well have specific meaning for *you* as well, because Jesus is *your* shepherd also, and you are one of his precious sheep!

JESUS, THE RESURRECTION AND THE LIFE

CHAPTER 11

Chapter 11 introduces us to three important characters in John's Gospel, all of whom were very special to Jesus during his earthly ministry. These people were Lazarus, Mary, and Martha—a brother and his two sisters. The chapter begins by telling us that Lazarus was sick.

Chapter 11, verse 3, says that the two sisters sent word to Jesus saying, "Lord, our brother Lazarus, the one you love, is very sick." Verse 5 says, "Jesus loved Martha and her sister and Lazarus." And in verse 11, Jesus called Lazarus "his friend." The four of them weren't just acquaintances. These were Jesus' close friends.

This family was well-to-do and lived in a larger home in Bethany, a small city about two miles east of Jerusalem. Jesus and his disciples chose this family's home to stay in when they visited Jerusalem. They felt very comfortable and at ease there. It was their home away from home, where they experienced warmth, love, and exceptional hospitality.

But on this occasion, there was a crisis. Lazarus had become very sick.

The sisters, knowing Jesus was in the area, sent word for him to come to them. We find in verses 21, 22, and 32 that they had the expectation that if Jesus had come, he could have healed Lazarus.

But when Jesus received word from Mary and Martha, instead of going to them right away, he stayed where he was two days longer. Then, while talking to his disciples, he informed them that Lazarus had died. By the time Jesus finally did arrive in Bethany, Lazarus had been in the tomb for four days. Jesus deliberately avoided the funeral and was absent when the other mourners came to comfort the sisters in their grief.

Somewhat strange and unexpected behavior on Jesus' part, no? Is this the way someone would normally respond to those he loves; to those who were among his closest friends on earth? More to the point: Is this the way we would expect God to treat his friends?

When Jesus finally arrived, you can tell by what both sisters said to him that they were disappointed he hadn't come sooner: "Lord, if You had been here, my brother would not have died." They wanted Jesus to heal Lazarus from his sickness. But what they didn't know was that Jesus wanted to do something even greater. Jesus wanted to raise him from the dead!

Jesus said to Martha, "Your brother will rise again."

Martha said to him, "I know that he will rise again in the resurrection on the last day."

Then Jesus dropped another "I am" truth bomb equivalent to a nuclear blast.

He said to her, "*I am* the resurrection and the life. He who believes in me will live even if he dies" (*emphasis mine*).

Mary's theology saw the resurrection in terms of some future event. But Jesus was telling her, "Yes, I'll be there on the last day to raise Lazarus up, but *I'm here right now* and that resurrection power that is in me is available for Lazarus right now!"

Jesus then sent Martha away and told her to tell Mary that he wanted to see her. Mary came and told him the same exact thing Martha did: "Lord, if You had been there, my brother would not have died." But Mary did something that Martha didn't do. Mary fell at his feet. (v.32)

Martha was a doer, a worker, and a server. Mary was a receiver, a responder and a worshipper. Martha took the initiative to go out to meet Jesus. Mary waited for Jesus to call her. Every time Mary appears in the Bible we see her at Jesus' feet—receiving his teaching, honoring him, or pouring out her love.

Jesus asked Mary and the others to take him to Lazarus's tomb. He was overcome by their grief. Tears streamed down his cheeks. Here, we read the shortest sentence in the Bible: Jesus wept. As God, he had the power to do anything. As a man, he wept.

Jesus approached the cave where a stone had been rolled in front of Lazarus' tomb. Remember, it had been four days since Lazarus had died. In the warm, Mediterranean climate, the body had already begun to decompose. When Jesus told them to roll the stone away, Martha protested because she knew there would be a stench. Still, they obeyed his command.

Then Jesus hollered at the top of his lungs, "Lazarus, come out!" (HCSB)

Momentarily, a body wrapped from head to toe in layered strips of linen grave clothes inched its way, shuffling slowly, out of the cave. Jesus had just brought a dead man back to life.

For those he loves, sometimes God doesn't answer prayers right away. But some things are worth waiting for. Sometimes he delays answering so that he can test our faith and give us an even greater revelation of himself.

Both the Old and the New Testaments teach that there will be a resurrection from the dead. It will be universal—everyone will be raised. The resurrection precedes a final judgment of the just and the unjust. On the last day, the God of creation will raise every person from the dead to stand before him and give an account.

How the resurrection on the last day will take place, we don't know for sure. Like many other things in the Bible, it is a mystery. The Bible does give some details, though. Jesus was the prototype—the first one to be resurrected from the dead. He takes first place in everything! So we can learn some things *his* resurrection.

Up until then, Mary and Martha, as well as Jesus' other followers, only knew Jesus as a healer. But Jesus wanted to reveal himself to them in a much greater way—he was the Resurrection.

Technically, though Jesus raised Lazarus from the dead and brought him back to life, Lazarus didn't get the full upgrade we will all get on the last day. Like other humans, he would have to die again *before* he experienced the resurrection Jesus was talking about.

When God resurrected Jesus from the dead, he gave Jesus a new, spiritual body. In that body, he could appear and disappear, transition from the spiritual realm to the physical realm effortlessly, walk through walls, and still eat the physical food mortals eat. His body has an eternal, lifetime guarantee. It will never wear out. The wonderful news for those of us who believe is that at the resurrection we will be clothed in new bodies.

What those bodies will be like, we don't know. We haven't been given the complete owners' manual. But this we do know: John gives us all we need to know in one of his other letters: "Dear friends, we are God's children now, and what we will be has not yet been revealed. We know that when He appears, we will be like Him because we will see Him as He is" (1 John 3:2 HCSB).

Jesus—the God-man who rejoiced with Lazarus, Mary, and Martha—loved them and gave them a taste of what *that day* will be like.

He *is* the resurrection and the life. He has the power to raise the dead, restore life, and on the last day he will be revealed as *the* Resurrection. When you die, it will be just like blinking. The light from this world will dim, but when you open your eyes, you will see Jesus and the wonderful realm of reality. You will be buried in the ground in your corrupted, natural body but raised with an incorruptible, glorious body, just like the one Jesus has. This same Jesus, who is the resurrection and the life, has now come to live in *your* spirit and is present with you right now.

And like Lazarus, Mary, and Martha, you are his friend. The same unfathomable, unchanging, unconditional, never-ending love he had them, he has for you as well!

What a God! What a gift!

Jesus, I Want to Love You Like That!

CHAPTER 12

John chapter 12 begins by telling us that six days before the Passover Jesus came again to Bethany. After Jesus raised Lazarus from the dead, he went from Bethany to a city called Ephraim and stayed there with his disciples because the Passover was near (John 11:54-55). Word of Lazarus being raised from the dead spread quickly. The chief priests and the Pharisees, who heard of this, were planning to seize Jesus and kill him, if they could find him (John 11:53, 57). Therefore, Jesus and his disciples retreated to the small city called Ephraim that was located in the hill country on the edge of the wilderness, approximately twelve to fifteen miles away, to wait before they went up to the feast. So all of these events—the raising of Lazarus and what we are about to look at in chapter 12 and what will follow—took place in the days and weeks shortly before Jesus' crucifixion.

The story begins with a supper. Jesus and his disciples (including Judas Iscariot, the one who would betray him) were all there, as well as his close friends, Lazarus, Mary, and Martha. Lazarus was kicked back in a recliner with Jesus, and Martha was serving. But the story focuses on Mary.

Supplementary information about this story appears in Matthew, Mark, and Luke's Gospels. (Different gospel accounts often add different particulars to the same story.) According to Mark, this supper actually occurred two days prior to the Passover (Mark 14:1). It was a dangerous time because the chief priests and the scribes were plotting how to seize Jesus by stealth and kill him (see also Matthew 26:4).

Both Matthew and Mark mention that this dinner took place at the home of Simon the leper.

You see, not only was Bethany the place where Jesus would go to hang out with his friends; it also had another reputation. The word "Bethany" means "House of Misery." Bethany was home to the closest leper colony to Jerusalem.

In those days, people believed that leprosy was spread by the wind. So the lepers were made to stay in Bethany because that's the direction the wind blew. If they were found outside of the boundaries designated for them, they could receive forty lashes.

Jewish rabbis had their own laws (here we go again—back to those oral traditions!) about how close they could get to lepers. If the wind was not blowing, they could get within six feet. If the wind was blowing, they were not supposed to get within 150 feet downwind of them.

But, praise God, Jesus was not like those rabbis. He ate with the lepers, touched them, and showed them genuine love and compassion. He was no stranger to those who called misery their home.

Now that all the characters are in place, let's move on to this precious story of what Mary did.

For some time, Jesus had been telling his disciples that he must go to

Jerusalem to suffer and die, but they could never really get their heads around this and accept it. Even up until this very time—two days before his crucifixion—they were living in a state of denial.

We learn from Matthew (26:2) that earlier that day Jesus told his disciples again that in two days the Son of Man would be betrayed and handed over to be crucified. Though the disciples were in denial, Mary was undone, panic-stricken. This was her Lord! This was the one she worshipped. And this night might be the last time she would ever see the one she loved so much!

Mary was the only one among them all that believed what Jesus had said and took him at his word.

What could she do?

She needed to do something to show him how much she loved him—how much he meant to her. All she could think about was her most valued possession—an alabaster vial containing a pound of very expensive perfume. It was her life savings—worth far more than a year's wages for an individual. But it meant nothing to her in comparison to Jesus. If he was going to die, then she would gladly use it all to anoint him for burial.

She took that vial with her into the middle of the dinner party—she didn't care what the others may have thought—and began pouring the precious perfume on Jesus' head (Matthew 26:7). Eyes of adoring love must have looked through tears into Jesus' eyes, as the oily perfume ran down from his head onto his face.

Then she fell to the floor and poured the remaining perfume on his feet (John 12:3) and began wiping them with her hair. The whole house filled with the fragrance of the perfume.

Judas looked on her extravagant act of love with contempt. "Why was this perfume not sold for three hundred denarii and given to poor people?" Not that he was interested in the poor—he was a thief and pilfered from the moneybox. All he saw was an opportunity to enhance his own investment portfolio.

John's account of this story ends with Jesus telling Judas to let her alone: "For you always have the poor with you, but you do not always have Me." But that was not the end of the story. Matthew's Gospel provides a dramatic exclamation point before bringing the story to a full close.

Matthew 26:13 records Jesus saying, "I promise you that wherever this gospel is preached in the whole world, this woman's extravagant devotion to Me will be mentioned in memory of her."

- When Mary poured out her all for Jesus, it gave off a fragrance that affected everyone in the room.
- Extravagant worship is part of the gospel message.
- Jesus memorializes those guilty of extravagantly worshipping him.
- True to Jesus' word, the fragrance of what Mary did has spread throughout the whole world as untold millions have read in the inspired gospel accounts of her devotion to Christ.

Oh Jesus, I want to love you like that!

DAY 42

THE HOUR HAS COME

CHAPTER 12

We'll be pushing off from the dock of the shallow waters of God this morning (if there are any shallow waters in God), catching a trade wind, and moving out into the deep. The next several chapters in John contain truth and revelation that can be difficult to understand, let alone explain. As rich as the revelation of Jesus we have seen up this point has been, for me, it's like everything prior was grade school, high school, or maybe college-level stuff. Now, as we move into chapter 12 and continue on through chapter 17, we're coming to the Master's, Doctorate, and Post-Doctorate material. This is exciting, but also challenging.

So, I find it appropriate at this time to steal another line from the Matrix once again: "Buckle your seat belt, Dorothy! Kansas is going bye-bye!"

Chapter 12 brings us to the end of Jesus' public ministry. It is a pivotal chapter that leads us into the final, intimate hours he spent with his disciples before going to the cross.

The turning point comes in chapter 12, verses 20-23:

> Now there were some Greeks [Gentiles—non-Jews]

among those who were going up to worship at the feast. These came to Philip, who was from Bethsaida of Galilee, and began to ask him, saying, "Sir, we wish to see Jesus."

Philip came and told Andrew; Andrew and Philip came and told Jesus. And Jesus answered them, saying, "The hour has come for the Son of Man to be glorified."

In verse 27, Jesus continues, "Now My soul has become troubled; and what shall I say, 'Father, save Me from this hour?' But for this purpose I came to this hour. Father, glorify Your name."

What did he mean when he said, "The hour has come?"

Earlier, at the wedding in Cana, when Jesus' mother told him the wedding party had run out of wine, Jesus said to her, "My hour has not come." At various other times, the religious leaders picked up stones to stone Jesus but he eluded them because, John says, "his hour had not come."

But now Jesus says, "My hour *has* come!" What hour was he speaking of?

The difficulty explaining this lies in the fact that different Scriptures attach different meanings to this "hour."

For instance, this passage in John 12 says that the hour for Jesus to be glorified had come. But there are also passages elsewhere in John that say something different. Here are some other places referring to "the hour," or the time that had come:

- Also in chapter 12, referring to "the hour," Jesus said, "Now the ruler of this world [Satan] will be cast out" (verse 31).
- Again, referring to "the hour": "And if I am lifted up from the earth [on the cross], I will draw all men to Myself" (verse 32).

- "Jesus knew that His hour had come to depart from this world to the Father. Having loved His own who were in the world, He loved them to the end . . . . He got up from supper, laid aside His robe, took a towel . . . and began to wash His disciples' feet" (John 13:1-5 HCSB).
- "The time has come when you will all be scattered, and each one of you will go your own way, leaving me alone! Yet I am never alone, for the Father is always with me" (John 16:32).
- "Father, the time has come. Unveil the glorious splendor of your Son so that I will magnify your glory! You have already given me authority over all people so that I may give the gift of eternal life to all those that you have given me" (John 17:1-2 TPT).

Then from Mark's Gospel we see this phrase again:

"The hour has come; behold, the Son of Man is being betrayed into the hands of sinners."
MARK 14:41

And in Luke, we see it once more:

"When the hour had come, He reclined at the table and the apostles with Him and He said to them, 'I have earnestly desired to eat this Passover with you before I suffer . . .' And when He had taken a cup [of wine] and given thanks, He said, 'Take this and share it among yourselves.'"
LUKE 22:14-20

It was at that hour that he shared a cup of wine and some bread with his disciples, instituting the New Covenant (agreement) with them, through the shedding of his blood. This is often referred to as the Lord's Supper, communion, or the Eucharist.

From all these references, we can conclude that this "hour" had to do with Jesus being glorified, casting out the ruler of this world, dying on the cross, drawing all men to himself, departing to the Father, loving his own until the end, his disciples being scattered, and not only Jesus being glorified, but his Father being glorified.

So how do we pull this all together so we can look through the wide-angle lens to see what it means?

Let me try to sum it up this way:

In the Book of Hebrews (chapter 12, verse 2) we are told to "fix our eyes on Jesus . . . who *for the joy set before Him* endured the cross, despising the shame. . . ." *(emphasis mine)*.

All the things that Jesus went through and endured—being misunderstood and rejected, suffering death on the cross to take away our sins—was for one purpose. It was for the *joy* that was set before him! This was the expectant joy that he had within himself from eternity past that motivated him to create. This was the joy of having a bride, a counterpart, a "corporate someone" taken from his creation that he could pour his love out on and who could become one with him, know him, enjoy him, and co-exist with him forever and ever. This was God's eternal purpose. This joy was Jesus' anticipation of receiving the gift the Father purposed to give him. That gift was his people—you and me and all those that have been called out of this world to take the rest of eternity to discover the unfathomable riches of knowing him.

When Jesus said, "My hour has come," he was looking ahead at the cost, the price he would have to pay, in order to spend an eternity loving on us, and being loved in return.

In the Old Testament, in the book entitled the Song of Solomon, King Solomon expresses his love for his bride in this way"

> You have made my heart beat faster, my sister, my bride;
> you have made my heart beat faster with a
> single glance of your eyes, with a single strand of your
> necklace. How beautiful is your love, my sister, my
> bride! How much better is your love than wine, and the
> fragrance of your oils than all kinds of spices!
> SONG OF SOLOMON 4:9-10

In these inadequate words, we see something of the heart of Jesus for his bride, and how this "hour that has now come" would quickly pass into eternal bliss.

JESUS, THE SEED

CHAPTER 12

When Jesus heard that the Greeks had come wanting to see him, the narrative changed. For three-and-a-half years he had roamed the land of Palestine, teaching and preaching to the Jews, with an occasional Gentile thrown in here and there. But this was like an alarm going off inside of him.

Jesus must have thought, "What? The Greeks are asking about me? They want to see me? There's an entire world out there beyond Judea, Samaria, and Galilee, in which I've been confined (with brief exceptions) these past thirty-three years. And that world is filled with Gentiles whom I love—Greeks, Romans, Persians, Asians, Egyptians, Arabs (and seeing into the future with all-knowing, all seeing eyes), Thai, Russians, Tibetans, Latinos, Zambians, and Americans. Confined to this body, as I am, there's only one way for the world to see me. It's time that, like a grain of wheat that falls into the earth and dies, I face the cross and end my earthly sojourn. Only then will I be able to draw people from all nations, all tribes, and all tongues to myself. Now is the time for the Son of all mankind, the Son of all humanity, to be lifted up on the cross. For this purpose I have come to this hour. Father, bring it on!"

It's a sobering thought that Jesus *had* to be crucified. But how would that glorify him?

Think back to creation, when God filled the earth with all kinds of physical images that mirrored spiritual realities. There was physical water that pictured living water from a different realm that Jesus would give. There was earthly bread that pictured the living bread that came down from heaven. There were the sacrificial lambs that pictured the Lamb of God who would die for the sin of the world. Now Jesus reveals that he is a seed, represented by a grain of wheat. Unless that grain of wheat dies it will remain alone. But if it dies, it will produce many grains. All the many grains that it can produce display the glory of the seed.

In the Genesis account of creation, in chapter one, God says:

> "Let the earth bring forth grass, herbs yielding seed, and fruit trees yielding fruit *after their kind, with seed in it,* upon the earth"; and it was so. . . . And the earth brought forth grass, and herb yielding seed after its kind, and the tree yielding fruit, with seed in it, after its kind: and *God saw that it was good.* . . . And God said, "Let the waters teem with swarms of living creatures, and birds that fly above the earth. . . ." And God created great whales, and every living creature that moves, which the waters brought forth abundantly, *after their kind,* and every winged fowl after its kind: and *God saw that it was good.* . . . And God said, "Let the earth bring forth the living creature after its kind, cattle, and creeping thing, and beast of the earth after its kind"; and it was so. And God made the beast of the earth after its kind and cattle after their kind, and

everything that creeps upon the earth after its kind: and *God saw that it was good (emphasis mine).*

God shares a particular attribute with every seed that has ever been created. He saw that all of this reproduction—seed producing seed, beast producing beast, after *their own kind*—was good because he knew that one day Jesus would come from heaven to earth as a seed! Just like Jesus is *real* light, *real* water, and *real* bread, he is the *real* seed after which all seeds on earth are just a pattern or a shadow.

We learn from a physical seed that if it's planted in the earth and everything goes according to plan—if it has adequate water, nutrients from the soil, and warmth from the sun—then something amazing will happen. One seed will grow up to produce a great harvest. If you plant the seed from an apple tree into the ground, an apple tree will grow up, producing apples after its kind, just like the original. Just one apple, with many seeds inside, has the potential to produce many apple trees, and an abundant amount of fruit. The same is true with oranges, figs, tomatoes, and pomegranates.

We see the same thing among animal species. Sharks produce baby sharks that grow up to be sharks. Eagles produce baby eagles that grow up to be eagles. Cows produce baby cows that grow up to be cows. Monkeys produce baby monkeys that grow up to be monkeys. Humans produce baby humans that grow up to be humans.

This is a principle that God has woven into the fabric of the universe.

Now comes the BIG question. What if God were a seed? What kind of fruit, or offspring, would God's seed produce? What kind of fruit would glorify God?

A physical seed can remain in its original state for a year, for 200 years, or, in some cases, 2,000 years. But until it is planted in the earth and dies, it will remain alone. It will never bear fruit or produce "offspring" after its kind.

Jesus came to this earth as a seed. He had patiently waited for ages upon ages in eternity past, and for thousands of years since the creation, to be planted in the ground and die. Since he was a child, he had known that he had come to earth for this purpose. Now the hour had arrived for him to bear fruit and to be glorified.

God's eternal plan was to draw all those who would believe in him to himself. He would do this by planting his seed of life within the soil of the human heart. That was the only way the whole world would be able to "see Jesus."

God had come to earth and become a man in the person of Jesus. Jesus lived and then he died. He was buried, but then he rose from the dead and became the Life-giving Spirit so that he could give himself away and plant his life inside of us. He breathed his breath into his disciples and said, "Receive the Holy Spirit" (John 20:22). This God-man Jesus, who once walked *with* his disciples, had now come to live *inside* of them.

An acorn, once it falls into the earth, has the capacity within itself to grow into a huge oak tree. In the same way, by his Spirit, Jesus came into you as a seed. As a seed, he will begin to live *his life* in you, will grow in you, will bear fruit in you, and, ultimately, will reproduce himself (his peace, his patience, his love—his nature) in you!

What a mystery! Concealed for ages. Now revealed.

Look around next time you step outside. What do you see? Plants? Trees?

Are they real plants or trees or are they something else? What about that bowl of fruit on the kitchen counter? Real fruit, or something else?

Or the next time that you hold a grain of rice in your hand, taste an almond or a sunflower seed, or see an acorn on the ground: what are those things—*really?*

Just as you lifted your glass several coffee conversations ago and thanked God that the water you were drinking was not real water, but only a picture of real water, each time that you encounter any of these things that the Creator has placed in your environment, it could be a time to do something like that again. Before you pop that almond in your mouth or that cup of rice in the rice cooker, or when you see that beautiful rose bush with all its flowers in bloom or that fruit-laden apple tree, realize that these are wonderful reminders, fresh opportunities to pause and praise God for who Jesus is. "Dear Lord Jesus, I thank you that these seeds, bushes, and trees are not real. They are only pictures. Thank you that you are the *real* seed who died and is now planted in my heart. Thank you that just as it is sure that an apple seed will grow up to be an apple tree, I can believe that it is your purpose to fully form your life in me!"

Welcome to your doctorate study program in knowing God. You will never get a degree and graduate from this program. You will always be learning and discovering more of the riches of this Jesus who has come to live in you.

That is what you were created for!

FOLLOWING JESUS WHO LIVES INSIDE OF YOU AS SPIRIT

CHAPTER 12

Did you ever stop to think that Christians are unique among all the species of life in the universe? Every other life form only has one life. But Christians have two.

A donkey has donkey life. A crocodile has crocodile life. But Christians who have experienced the second birth are different. Not only do they have the sin-infected, human life that they were born with, but, once they are born again, they receive another life—divine life—when Jesus comes to live inside them.

Being a Christian is now a whole lot more complicated. That's where the difficulty comes in, figuring out how to live by this new life that you have received.

Immediately after Jesus said that he was a grain of wheat that needed to fall into the earth and die, he said this:

He who loves his life loses it, and he who hates his life in this world will keep it to life eternal. If anyone serves Me, he must follow Me; and where I am, there My servant will be also; if anyone serves Me, the Father will honor him.

JOHN 12:25-26

Here's my paraphrase for that passage:

"The person who wants to preserve the sinful, self-centered life that they inherited from Adam and have lived by since birth will lose out on the life that I have given them, the life I created them to live by. But the one who hates that old life, and is willing to reject it, can lay hold of the eternal life that I came to give them. If anyone wants to serve me, then they must follow my example and live the way I did. I lived by the life of the Father. They must learn to live by me."

I can almost hear you thinking, "Yeah, OK, I hear you. But just how am I supposed to do that?"

Let's start with the basics. Before Jesus came into your spirit and made you alive to God, you had no access to the heavenly Wi-Fi. You weren't picking up the signal on your end.

But now, his life *is* inside of you (in your spirit, to be specific). You just need to start learning how to find it.

As I mentioned earlier, the Bible teaches that God created us body, soul, and spirit (1 Thessalonians 5:23). Our bodies were created for us to have contact with the physical world; our souls, to have contact and relationship with other people and living things; and our spirits, to contact and have relationship with God.

Besides creating you with a spirit, God made you with a soul to express the unique personality he has given you. In all of us, over time, those personalities get out of whack for all kinds of reasons: growing up in dysfunctional families, living "privileged" lives, experiencing tragedies, and so forth.

A part of your soul is your emotions. God gave you emotions so that you could experience different feelings. But some people learn to rely too heavily on those feelings—in fact, become governed by them. For example, someone might say, "It's dreary and overcast today. That makes me sad, so I'm going to be sad today." Or, "I'm feeling angry, so I'll just express that anger, without thinking first about the consequences."

Feelings can fluctuate depending on your circumstances and can't always be trusted. You may feel rejected by a friend through misinterpreting something they wrote in an email, but that may not have been what they intended to communicate at all. Feelings can either reinforce what is true, or result in you believing lies.

The same is true of your thoughts. Satan, God's enemy, is called the accuser. Sometimes you may be aware of a voice inside your head accusing you of different things, intending for you to believe lies. Thoughts like, *You are really stupid. You are ugly. You are such a failure. Your opinions are not worth listening to, so just shut up. Nobody really cares what you think anyway. You could never do that.* So on, and so on.

God doesn't think you are stupid; he is pleased with you. God doesn't think you are ugly; he sees you as his righteous, holy, and beautiful child. No matter how many times you have failed, God sees you as forgiven. He doesn't see you as one with no future. He sees you as his trophy, like a racecar with an engine under the hood that is more powerful than you can even imagine.

Another part of your personality is your will. You may have an overly developed, strong will that is able to force almost anything you want to achieve into existence. Or your will may be weak: more susceptible to giving up, not finishing the task, or succumbing to temptation. We all have our strengths and our weaknesses.

But if we are to follow Jesus, we need to submit our wills to him—whether they are naturally strong or feeble. For instance, you might ask, "Jesus, this is what I really, really, really want to do, but is this your will?" Or, "Jesus, I know what you want me to do, but I feel weak. Strengthen and empower me to do *your* will."

The Apostle Paul said, "Therefore as you have received Christ Jesus the Lord, so walk in him" (Colossians 2:6). How did you receive him? By faith. How do you walk in him? You walk in him the same way, by believing—believing what is true and rejecting the lies.

Judging other people comes very naturally; it is just part of our fallen human natures. A person will walk into a room and automatically begin sizing up the people there. That one is pretty. That one is stupid. That one is arrogant. That one is pretty ugly, arrogant, *and* stupid! That woman talks too much. That man is a liar. That person is worthless, etc. In addition, we compare ourselves to others, putting ourselves on some scale either above them or beneath them.

But how did Jesus judge people? How did he see the sinful Samaritan woman, Nicodemus, the adulterous woman, or the invalid man at the pool? He saw them as broken, empty, and needy, people just living their lives as best as they could while deep down inside they were hurting and searching, looking for something that would satisfy their deepest needs.

Jesus showed them compassion. He was full of grace for them (an extravagant generosity to give beyond anything they deserved), and offered them truth. Now *that* life is in you! Find it. Draw upon it. Live it.

Another example of needing to reject our old lives can be seen in people with a victim mentality. Many people develop a negative self-assessment that, over the years, causes them to always see themselves as victims. Their lives are full of self-pity, which really amounts to idolatry, because they think so much about themselves that they cannot whole-heartedly worship God or love others. They worship themselves instead. People caught in this trap must learn to recognize that always seeing yourself as a victim, having no power to overcome your circumstances, is a lie that comes directly from the enemy— Satan. Those lies, thoughts, and that old life needs to be rejected. Learning to look to Jesus and replacing those old thoughts with what God says is true about you is the answer.

Jesus says that you are forgiven, you are holy, you are blameless, you are beloved in his sight, you have purpose, and you have strength through the new life that he has given you to live a victorious life. Exercise faith. Build some new spiritual muscles. Is that sin-infected, fallen, self-centered old life the kind of life Jesus wants you to live? Think about it. Do you think Jesus was willing to endure the cross, suffer the pain, and give you his life just so you could remain stuck in that rut? Come on!

Opposite from the victim mentality are those with superiority complexes. They think of themselves as superior to others and live their lives accordingly. This is part of the old human nature as well, and also needs to be rejected. Jesus, who is God and who is superior in every way to all of us, came as a servant. That life is now living in you. Find it.

We all, at one time or another, have taken on false identities. Some of those identities can be very negative and crippling, for instance the person who sees him or her self as an alcoholic, a drug addict, a sexual pervert, a thief, or a glutton, etc. Whatever label like that you may have taken on and attached to yourself in the past needs to be rejected. Deny that identity because in the eyes of God, it no longer exists. That is not who *you are!* Jesus has given you a new identity. You are a child of God! You are part of the bride of Christ—loved and cherished! Latch onto it by faith. Faith is your exit off the freeway going nowhere. Simply believing that what God says about you is true and rejecting lies and false identities is the way to freedom and realizing your *true* identity. Sometimes that requires rolling up your sleeves and going to war against the lies. But with practice, it becomes easier.

On another front, God may have given you talents such as being a good writer, an athlete, an artist, a factory worker, or a computer technician—all of which are good things. But if those are the identities from which you derive your self-worth, that needs to be rejected as well. God's love for you does not depend on how well you perform in any particular field or endeavor; God loves you just because he loves you. It's that simple. You are pleasing to him. It is his nature to love, and that love is unconditional. Trying to earn his love through any performance-based merit system is also part of that old life that needs to be rejected.

In the film *The Matrix*, Neo took the red pill and discovered a whole new reality. But he also quickly learned that before he could fully enter into his new identity and discover who he was intended to be, he had to go through some training.

This is where you are. You are now in training. Your new assignment: continue to learn to reject that old, broken life that was once so natural for you to live, and lay hold of your new life. You are a child of God. You are a friend of God. You are beloved of God. By denying that old life and learning to live by the new life Jesus has given you, you will experience your new identity and all that you were intended to be!

JESUS, THE SERVANT

CHAPTER 13

By the end of chapter 12, Jesus' public ministry had come to an end. Knowing that his time to face the cross had come, he spent his final hours on earth with those closest to him. Chapters 13 through 17 record the last meal (known as the Last Supper) they would have together. This was a very intimate time. During this meal, things that weighed heaviest on Jesus' heart—the last drops of teaching, instruction, comfort, and demonstrations of love—would be poured out.

As John penned the very first verse of chapter thirteen, it seems his most vivid impression of his and the other disciple's entire experience with Jesus was how much Jesus had loved them. If John were to have made it totally personal instead of general, he would have expressed what was written in that first verse this way: "... Jesus, knowing that his hour had come that he would depart out of this world to the Father, having loved those of us who were with him in the world, he loved us right up until the very end."

By this time the twelve had followed Jesus for the better part of three-and-a-half years. With all they'd seen and heard, there was so much that they still didn't understand. They had heard his teaching. They had seen Jesus heal the sick, give sight to the blind, and feed the 5,000. They knew that when they traveled together, the coins in the moneybag they carried were not only used to meet their own needs, but also to feed the poor. But with all the teaching they had received and all the demonstrations of Jesus' miracles, power, and love they had seen, they were still pretty dense when it came to understanding spiritual things. But that did not stop Jesus from delivering, in these final hours, some of the greatest bombshell revelations that they would ever hear from his lips. Truly, Jesus had saved the best wine for last.

The chapter begins with the story of a foot washing.

The story behind the story of foot washing is this: In those days, the poor mostly walked around barefooted. Those that had the money would buy or make open-faced sandals consisting of a sole and two leather straps, one overlaying the foot and the other around the heel.

It didn't take long walking on the dusty roads and pathways, or working in the fields, for a person to accumulate a layer of dirt on their feet. So upon entering a home at the end of the day it was customary for people to have their feet washed, usually by slaves or servants. Those who received foot washing from another were considered to be socially superior to the one who performed the task. It was done out of honor and respect.

A Jewish man would normally accept foot washing only from his own slave, his wife, or his children. Also, the relationship of students to Jewish rabbis was similar to that of a slave to his master. Whatever duties a slave would perform for their master, a pupil would do for the rabbi. This would include foot washing.

With that in mind, let's look at the account of how Jesus washed the disciples' feet.

Jesus "got up from supper, laid aside His robe, took a towel, and tied it around Himself. Next, He poured water into a basin and began to wash His disciples' feet and to dry them with the towel tied around Him" (John 13:4-5 HCSB). By doing this, Jesus took the form of a servant.

When he came to Peter, Peter's reaction was at first one of bewilderment. "Lord, are You going to wash *my* feet?"

Jesus told Peter that he wouldn't understand this now, but later he would.

Having Jesus wash his feet came as an incomprehensible shock to Peter. He was looking at Jesus' actions through the eyes of a traditional Jew. This was so radical. He was unable to bear it!

What he said next does not come across as strongly in most texts as in the original. In protest, Peter blurted out something like this to Jesus: "No, Lord! Never in a million years shall you wash my feet!"

Peter's stubborn theology was about to go up in smoke. For him, all of this was backwards. After all that time he'd spent with Jesus, he thought he'd finally figured this thing with Jesus out: Jesus was the Lord and Master; Peter was the servant. Jesus had waited until this moment—just hours before the cross—to give Peter, and the other disciples, an even higher revelation.

Looking back, Jesus had already spoken directly to his disciples on the subject of leaders and servants. In Mark 10:42-45 Jesus had told them this:

> You know that those who are recognized as rulers of the

Gentiles lord it over them; and their great men exercise authority over them. But it is not this way among you, but whoever wishes to become great among you shall be your servant and whoever wishes to be first among you shall be slave to all. For even the Son of Man did not come to be served, but to serve, and to give His life a ransom for all.

It still didn't click for Peter (or for the other apostles, for that matter) then. It wasn't until after the cross that a broken and humiliated Peter, a much more humble and receptive man, would understand the extent to which Jesus came as a servant, and the lengths that a servant would go to serve those he loves.

There is more to this story that we'll pick up tomorrow. But in the meantime, think on this: The God of the universe who loved you so much that he was willing to die for you, did not save you so that you could serve him, he saved you so that he could serve you!

SEEING JESUS THROUGH NEW EYES

CHAPTER 13

We're only partway into the story of the night that Jesus washed his disciples' feet. The consequences stemming from this revelation that Jesus came to serve, rather than to be served, have far-reaching implications for what *our* attitude toward God should be.

Following Peter's adamant protest, Jesus' dialogue with him continued:

> Jesus answered him, "If I do not wash you, you have no part with Me."
>
> Simon Peter said to him, "Lord, then wash not only my feet, but also my hands and my head."
>
> Jesus said to him, "He who has bathed needs only to wash his feet, but is completely clean; and you are clean, but not all of you" [referring to Judas, who would betray him].
> JOHN 13:8-10

If I could paraphrase what Jesus was saying, it would go something like this: "Peter, if you want to have any part in this ministry I have called you to, then you are going to have to learn that you will never be able to serve others unless you first let me serve you.

"Once you wash, you are clean. I am going to completely wash you and clean away every one of your sins when I go to the cross. But you are still going to be living in this world. As you walk through this world, you will not be able to avoid accumulating dust on your feet. You will not be able to escape being around people that engage in filthy conversation, or hear things you don't want to hear that will affect your mind, or see things that you don't want to see that will affect your heart. You will need to spend time with me, letting me serve you, letting me wash that dust off your feet, letting me speak to you, letting me encourage and strengthen you, so that you will be refreshed and renewed. Only then will you be able to serve others.

"You see, Peter, your spiritual reserve is like a pitcher of water within you. At times that water level will get low. But I will always be here to refill it. Understand this, Peter: just as the flowers were created to lift their heads in response to the warmth of the sun's rays, so you too were created to respond to me. I am the giver; you are the receiver.

"Only when you learn to be a receiver and let me fill you up will you then become a giver, and be able to wash the feet of others."

Later, Jesus told Peter, "Truly, truly I say to you, a slave is not greater than his master, nor is the one who is sent greater than the one who sent him" (John 13:16). Clearly, Jesus fully intended to send Peter and the other apostles out as his ambassadors, his apostles. But first, they needed to learn this valuable lesson.

When I think of the context of this verse, where Jesus spoke about sending them out with the gospel message, and its context of foot washing, it reminds me of Isaiah 52:7, a verse that also mentions feet: "How beautiful on the mountains are the feet of him who brings good news, who announces peace, and brings good news of happiness, who announces salvation, and says to Zion, 'Your God reigns!'"

Those who are sent out with the gospel message have clean feet, beautiful feet.

Finally, I think there is another application we can draw from this passage.

About thirty years later, chained to a Roman guard while under house arrest in Rome, the Apostle Paul wrote a letter to a church he had started in Ephesus (modern-day Turkey). Paul had experienced Jesus as the seed who went into the earth and died, then rose again, and now had come to live in him. The same Jesus who had revealed himself as the Servant at the Last Supper, was now, through the Spirit, bearing fruit after his kind in Paul. In his letter, Paul was giving instructions about the husband-wife relationship and wrote this:

> Husbands, love your wives, just as Christ also loved
> the church and gave Himself up for her, so that He
> might sanctify her [set her apart], having *cleansed* her
> *by the washing of water with the word*, that He might
> present to Himself the church in all her glory, having
> no spot or wrinkle or any such thing; but that she
> would be holy and blameless. So ought husbands also
> to love their own wives ...
> EPHESIANS 5:25-28, *emphasis mine.*

Can you see the same Savior-Servant you read about in John chapter 13 here? Jesus hasn't changed. He still has the same servant heart for his church and for you and me today. He loves you. He gave himself for you. He chose you, he found you, he called you when you were just a common, ordinary, lost sinner, and he is making you extraordinary by lifting you up to the highest place of honor and respect. He cleansed you and washed you. As a result, you are glorious and radiant in his eyes. And because he is holy, he made you holy and blameless as well.

Yes, God is king, but he is unlike the kings of this world. He is a servant king. He doesn't coerce or rule by force. His love is so strong, so powerful, so magnetic, that the more you understand and experience it, the more you will be drawn to him and become love's willing prisoner. No force in the universe can compare with the power of God's love.

Dear friend, be the receiver you were intended to be. Come before Jesus with a humble heart and open hands and allow him to be the giver in your life. He has an unlimited supply of grace, truth, and love to pour out on you!

TENSION & ANXIETY IN THE UPPER ROOM

CHAPTER 13

Wonder, tension, and anxiety intertwined that night in the upper room where Jesus and his disciples took their last meal together.

Ever since Leonardo Da Vinci released his classic painting "The Last Supper," this meal in the upper room has been known by that name. (In case you're interested, that happened sometime shortly after Columbus discovered America.) But was it the *Last* Supper? Not really.

To be more accurate, the Passover meal that Jesus took with his disciples that night should really be titled something like, "The Last of 1,500 Years of Picture Passover Suppers." Jesus fulfilled the picture and became our Passover Lamb. From that point forward in history there would be no need to celebrate the picture any longer. The reality had come. Additionally, the Book of Acts (10:40) records that Jesus appeared to his disciples after his resurrection and that they "ate and drank with him," so this wasn't Jesus' "last supper" ever with his disciples.

That being said, this was the final meal Jesus ate with them before his death. According to Mark's Gospel, this meal took place in an upper room. Many scholars believe this was the guest room of an Essene monastery located in Jerusalem. (Yep, that was the same group that raised John the Baptizer out in the wilderness.) The Essenes were known for their hospitality.

In those days, the job of fetching and carrying water was something reserved for women, girls, and young boys—not for men. However, Jesus had instructed his disciples to look for a man carrying water, who would lead them to the place where they would prepare this last Passover meal (Luke 22:7-13). Most likely this was an Essene.

When I began this coffee conversation I used the word "wonder" because Jesus did not share some of his deepest teachings with his disciples until that night. But I also mentioned tension and anxiety. Why?

First of all, the disciples knew that a hostile crowd of religious leaders and Jews were lurking somewhere outside with plans to kill Jesus. They were worried and frightened. Secondly, no sooner had Jesus finished his wonderful demonstration and teaching about being a servant, than he revealed that one of his disciples would soon betray him. The disciples turned to one another, wondering who Jesus could be talking about. Blood pressures began to rise.

Then Jesus told them that he must go away and that where he was going they could not come. It finally dawned on them that Jesus was stone-cold serious. The one they loved was *really* going to leave them. This was even more reason for them to become deeply distressed.

But sandwiched between it all, Jesus shared a new commandment with them that they probably barely heard or understood at the time because they were so distracted by their growing concerns. This truth, however, would soon become characteristic of their relationships together and create a ripple effect around the world.

Jesus began by calling them "little children," a term of endearment, because at that point they still were little children in their understanding. "Little children, I am with you a little while longer. You will seek Me; and as I said to the Jews, now I say to you, 'Where I am going, you cannot come.' A new commandment I give to you, that you love one another, even as I have loved you, that you also love one another. By this all men [everyone] will know that you are My disciples."(John 13:33-35)

Peter, as was normally the case, just couldn't hold back and interrupted with a question: "Lord, where are you going?"

Jesus' answer, Peter's response, and then a strong word from Jesus to Peter ended the chapter. Unfortunately, at this point, we're going to need to abandon the story until tomorrow. For at this juncture, the translators that translated the Bible committed one of the most flagrant personal fouls in the history of translating. Yellow flags should have gone up all over the place. Peter's question and Jesus' answer was interrupted by the two short, but devastating words: "Chapter 14."

Because this passage of Scripture was truncated by the insertion of a new chapter heading that was not in the original language, we have been severed from understanding one of the most precious truths a troubled believer would ever want to hear.

JESUS, THE REMEDY FOR TROUBLED HEARTS

CHAPTER 14

Let's pick up the story again as if there had been replay cameras filming this foul on the part of the translators, but the refs caught the infraction and gave us a do-over.

Peter was obviously getting more and more troubled. His ego had already taken a big hit when he was singled out as the ignoramus in the room who had tried to prevent Jesus from washing his feet. Hearing that there was a traitor among them added more angst to the confusion brewing in Peter's heart. But this was not the half of it. What came next sidelined Peter and took him out of the game completely.

Peter's dialogue with Jesus went like this:

> Peter: Where are you going?
>
> Jesus: Where I am going you cannot follow me now. But you will follow me later.
>
> Peter: Lord, why can't I follow you right now? I will lay down my life for you.

Jesus: Will you really lay down your life for me? I'm telling you that a rooster will not crow until you deny me three times.

Heart-wrenching for self-confident Peter! With that answer chapter 13 ends. Last seen, we see poor Peter left sinking in the pit of despair.

If we were to just continue merrily along reading our Bibles, we'd pick up again in John chapter 14, verse 1: "Do not let your heart be troubled; believe in God, believe also in Me." We would be led to think of this like the next act of a play: the curtains had closed and reopened, the old props had been removed and replaced with new ones.

But no! That is not the way the original passage was written.

In chapter 14 (which never should have been a new chapter), Jesus continued his discussion with Peter. It had never ended.

Jesus had just told Peter that he was going to deny him three times. Peter was crushed. But on the heels of that, Jesus added,

> Do not let your heart be troubled; believe in God, believe
> also in Me. In My Father's house are many dwelling
> places; if it were not so, I would have told you; for I go to
> prepare a place for you. If I go and prepare a place for you,
> I will come again and receive you to Myself, that where I
> am, you may be also. And you know the way where I am
> going.
> JOHN 14:1-3

In today's jargon, here is what Jesus was saying to Peter:

"Don't worry about it, Peter. I've got your back. You denying me doesn't change anything. I know what you are capable of doing, even though you don't really know yourself yet. You've still got to learn to not trust in yourself. But trust in me! Everything is under control. I know that you are going to betray me. But I'm going to prepare a place for you in my Father that is so out of this world, you wouldn't believe it even if I told you. Chin up, Peter! It's OK. Yes, you'll deny me three times. But don't despair. Don't let your heart be troubled. I'm not troubled over this. Just believe in God and believe in me, and that troubled heart of yours will be put to rest."

What a promise for a troubled heart! What a promise for the Christian who fears that he or she has done something so terrible that Jesus could never forgive them. If you knew yourself like Jesus knows you, you would know that all he ever expects from you is to fail. He never expected you to be able to live the Christian life on your own, in your own strength. He is the only one who has ever or will ever be able to live the Christian life, and *he* will do that in you. If you are stopping and starting, sputtering along like a car with old fuel in the tank, you need a new fill up. Peace and victory is in the fuel formula of the Spirit that has come to live inside of you. Change your fuel, and your engine will run perfectly, just the way it's supposed to.

Every time your heart is troubled about your performance or you are worried about past failures or what lies ahead, you have taken your eyes off of Jesus. Believe in Jesus. Trust in Jesus. He is the cure for all those with chronic, troubled-heart syndrome.

DAY 49

A CLASSROOM OF
TROUBLED HEARTS

CHAPTER 14

There were others in the fraternity of troubled hearts in the upper room that night. Peter wasn't the only one distressed by Jesus' words.

Before Peter could respond to Jesus' last statement, Thomas chimed in with a question of his own. He seemed to be troubled because he didn't think they got the answer to the question Peter had originally asked Jesus: "Lord, where are you going?"

Thomas asked, "Lord, we do not know where you are going, how do we know the way?" (John 14:5). (Obviously, he was a bit confused here because Jesus *did* say where he was going: he was going to the Father.)

Jesus answered, "*I am* the way, the truth, and the life; no one comes to the Father but through Me. If you had known Me, you would have known My Father also; from now on you know Him, and have seen Him" (John 14:6, *emphasis mine*).

Different question, same answer. The answer to Peter's question was, "Believe in Me." In response to Thomas's troubled heart question (How do we know the way?), Jesus answered the same, "I *am* the way."

In this classroom of confounded students, all of a sudden Philip raised his hand: "Lord, show us the Father and it is enough for us."

Jesus' response pointed right back to himself once more:

> Have I been so long with you, and yet you have not
> come to know Me, Philip? He who has seen Me has
> seen the Father; how can you say, 'Show us the Father?'
> Do you not believe that I am in the Father, and the
> Father is in Me? The words I say to you I do not speak
> on My own initiative, but the Father abiding in Me does
> his works.
>
> JOHN 14: 9-10

So far, in past coffee conversations, much has been said about God the Father living inside Jesus. But what did Jesus mean when he said, "I am in the Father *and* the Father is in Me?"

This is important because it has implications for how we should live.

God the Father, who is Spirit, lived within Jesus' spirit. That's "the Father is in Me." Jesus was continually turning to, living in, living by that Spirit. That's the "I am in the Father" part.

Later in the chapter Jesus said that he would ask the Father, and the Father would give us the Helper, the Spirit of truth that would be with us forever. Then he said, "In that day you will know that I am in the Father, and you in Me, and I in you" (John 14:20) and that "*We*" (Father and Son) will come to make their dwelling place with us.

We are to live just like Jesus. We have spirits. God the Father, Jesus, and the Spirit of truth have come to live in our spirits. As we continue to turn to, live in, and live by that Spirit, that is the "you in Me" part that Jesus was talking about.

This may sound complicated and your mind will never be able to satisfactorily dissect this and figure it all out. It is a mystery. Just believe that God is in Christ, Christ is in you, and he lives in you through the Spirit. Keep it as simple as that and look to Jesus.

Peter wanted to know where Jesus was going. Thomas not only wanted to know the destination, but he also wanted the road map for how to get there. For Philip, the question was more theological; it was about God: "Just show us the Father, then we'll be happy. We won't be troubled anymore" (paraphrase).

Jesus' answer to Philip was the same one he gave to Peter and Thomas. "Philip, if you've seen *Me*, you've *seen* the Father!" (paraphrase).

One more hand went up in the room that day, or, at least one more that we know of. It was the hand of Judas (not Judas Iscariot, who was to betray him—a different Judas). His question was, "Lord, what then has happened that You are going to disclose Yourself to us and not to the world?" (John 14:22).

Judas's mind had got hung up in the middle of Jesus' explanation to Philip, where Jesus said, "I will ask of the Father, and He will give you another Helper, that He may be with you forever; the Spirit of truth whom the world cannot receive, because it does not see Him or know Him, but you know Him because He abides with you and will be in you. I will not leave you as orphans; I will come to you" (John 14:16-18).

Of all the incredibly deep truth packed in those verses, Judas was pre-occupied with why Jesus was only going to disclose himself to them and not to the world. The answer for that is simple: only those that are Jesus' disciples and love Jesus receive the Holy Spirit. The world (unbelievers) do not.

Jesus ends this chapter with wonderful words of encouragement:

> But the Helper, the Holy Spirit, whom the Father will send in My name, he will teach you all things, and bring to your remembrance all that I said to you. Peace I give to you; not as the world gives do I give to you. Do not let your heart be troubled, nor let it be fearful. You heard that I said to you, "I go away, and I will come to you." If you loved Me, you would have rejoiced because I go to the Father, for the Father is greater than I. Now I have told you before it happens, so that when it happens, you may believe.
>
> JOHN 14:26-29

At the beginning of chapter 14 Jesus said, "Do not let your heart be troubled; believe in God, believe also in Me." Now as this conversation draws to a close, he wraps it up by saying the same thing, but adds something to it: "Do not let your heart be troubled, nor let it be fearful" (John 14:27).

Don't be troubled and don't be afraid.

The remedy for a troubled heart in verse 1 was, "Believe in God, believe also in Me."

The remedy for a troubled *and* fearful heart in verse 27 was the same, only stated a bit differently: "You have heard that I said to you, I will go away and I will come to you."

The remedy was, "I will come to you."

Whether your troubled heart comes from worry or anxiety, theological questions, doctrinal issues, circumstances or experiences, the cure for every troubled and fearful heart is the same. That cure is believing in Jesus, believing that he is God, knowing that he lives in perfect peace, and that he wants to give that peace to you because he has everything under control!

Many wonderful truths and questions from this incredible chapter remain to be explored. We'll get to more of it tomorrow!

The Spirit That Lives in You

CHAPTER 14

Before getting into any new material, let's have a brief review.

In this section, from chapters 13 to 17, John narrates the last hours that Jesus spent with his disciples while on earth. And what hours they were! In that brief span of time it was as if he carpet-bombed them with new truths, one after another. He may have hinted concerning some of these truths during his three-and-a-half years of ministry, but much of this they had never heard before and certainly had no time to process.

He revealed that he was the Servant and that they needed to wash one another's feet. He gave them a new commandment—to love one another just as he had loved them—and said that by their love, others would know they were his disciples.

He spoke to them about his Father's house, where he was going to prepare a place for them. He told them that if they had seen him, they had seen God. He also revealed himself to them as the heart doctor who was the cure for any troubled heart.

Then he talked about the Helper, the Spirit of truth, the Holy Spirit whom he would send (which we'll cover in this conversation). And he also talked with them about praying in his name—something they had never done before (which we'll cover in the next conversation).

What a night! And this was just for starters.

Earlier I mentioned that when we come to these chapters in John, we move into deep waters. This is Doctorate and Post-Doctorate study in understanding God and his ways. We're like high school math students dropping in on an Einstein lecture on the theory of relativity.

I think we sometimes give ourselves too much credit for being smart—as if we had the ability to explain God. But if we could explain God totally, then we would *be* God. That's just not going to happen.

In eternity we will constantly be in awe; we will always be learning and discovering more about who God is, who Jesus is. How can our finite words and limited vocabulary describe the wonder of the infinite God? They simply can't.

But this one thing I do know: the infinite God has chosen to reveal himself in Jesus Christ. And the way we can come to know Jesus is through the Holy Spirit.

In the final book of the Bible, Revelation, this same Apostle John was caught up in the Spirit—to that other realm—and given a revelation of eternity. He wrote that the glory of God will light up the city of God and the lamp is the Lamb (Jesus). That's in Revelation 21:23.

In human terms, think of it this way: imagine a lamp. When you turn on a lamp, you will not see the small wire filament or the gas or electricity inside that causes it to light up. All you will see is the bright, shining lamp. In the same way, the glory of God will eternally reside inside of Jesus Christ. Jesus is God's expression. Through Jesus, the glory of God will be seen. Jesus is the only way in which we will ever see the Father. Now, with that behind us, let's talk about the Holy Spirit.

Since you have been a Christian, you have no doubt heard people talk about the God of the Bible as the Trinity. He is the three in one—the Father, the Son, and the Holy Spirit. This is true. He is all of this. But the word "Trinity" is not in the Bible—no, not one time.

We do see different titles given to God, such as "the Father," the "Spirit of God," "the Spirit," "the Spirit of him who raised Jesus from the dead," "His Spirit"—particularly in books like Romans, chapter 8.

We also see different titles given to Jesus. He is called "the Lord," and "Lord Jesus." We read much in the New Testament about us being "in Christ," "in Christ Jesus," or "in Him," and that the Spirit of Christ is in us.

In Romans 8 we are told that "there is now no condemnation for those who are in Christ Jesus, for the law of the Spirit of life in Christ Jesus has set us free from the law of sin and death" (Romans 8:1-2). We also learn from 1 Corinthians 15:45 and 2 Corinthians that Jesus became the life-giving Spirit. 2 Corinthians 4:17 says, "*Now* the Lord is the Spirit, and where the Spirit of the Lord is, there is freedom" (*emphasis mine*).

Here in John chapter 14 we are now looking at the Holy Spirit. Other titles for the Holy Spirit are the "Helper" and the "Spirit of truth," who Jesus said the Father would send to his disciples, who would teach them and lead them into all truth.

In the same breath (referring to the Spirit of truth), Jesus told his disciples,

"You know Him because He abides *with you* and *will be in you. I* will not leave you as orphans; *I will come to you"* (John 14:17-18, *emphasis mine*). Then again in verse 28 he said, "You heard that I said to you, 'I go away, and *I will come to you.'* If you loved Me, you would have rejoiced because I go to the Father. . . " (*emphasis mine*).

I can see Peter wrinkling his brow and reasoning to himself, "So, the Holy Spirit is going to be in us *and* Jesus is going to come back and he'll be in us too? Just how is that going to happen?"

Gets a little confusing, doesn't it?

It is a mystery. Perhaps it is the greatest mystery that God has left us humans to contemplate until we see Jesus face to face.

Who actually *is* in you? Laying aside all the titles and names he is given, the answer is, "All of God is in you!"

That really is something to rejoice about!

Books have been written on the subjects of the Trinity and of the Holy Spirit. But if I could sum it up in its simplest terms, I would say it this way: God is in Christ, who is in you, through the Holy Spirit.

That's about as good as you'll get out of me. If you want more, you'll have to buy another book!

GREATER WORKS & PRAYING IN JESUS' NAME

CHAPTER 14

I want to wrap up John chapter 14 today. One particular passage that caught my attention is this one:

> In fact, I say to you, whoever[1] believes in Me will do the deeds that I do, and will actually do greater deeds than these, because I am going to the Father. And the things you ask in my Name, I will do, so that honor is brought to the Father by means of the Son. Whatever you ask me in my Name, I will certainly do.
>
> JOHN 14:12-14, THE SOURCE

What does "greater works" or "greater deeds" mean? Does that mean that we will do even more awesome, greater works than Jesus? We'll do even greater things than raising the dead? No, I don't think so. The servant is not

---

1   Many translations use the pronoun "he." "*He* who believes in me, the works that I do *he* will do also; and greater works than these will *he* do because I go to the Father." I used the Source translation of the New Testament by Dr. A. Nylan, a Greek scholar, just to make the point this is not a "men only" promise. The pronoun in the Greek is gender neutral. Women, you're included too!

greater than his master, and the one who is sent is not greater than the one who sends him. Greater, I believe, refers to more, as in greater in number.

Jesus was only on earth physically for a limited time, and could only do so much. Think of the countless miracles and good works Christians have done throughout the centuries and the harvest of miracles and good works that have been released because he was the seed who fell into the earth to die.

The other thing I want to touch briefly on is praying in Jesus' name.

This could turn out to be one of those coffee conversations where you need to go for refills several times. I don't want you to have to do that, so I'll try to keep it short and very simple.

First, I'll tell you what it's not. It's not a formula for how to end a prayer: ". . . in Jesus' name, amen." Jesus is not impressed with form, ritual, or mindless repetition. He looks at the heart.

The name of a person is equivalent to a person himself or herself. If you write a check and someone cashes it at the bank, the bank will honor it, because your name represents you. It stands for who you are.

You can think of a myriad of things to pray and ask God for. You can pray for your cat, that she sleeps well at night, or that God would give you a parking spot right in front of the store you want to shop at (which I have seen him do!). And you can end every prayer "in Jesus name, amen." But is this what Jesus meant when he said every prayer we pray in Jesus' name would be answered?

Praying in Jesus' name runs much deeper than that.

In 1 Corinthians 2:11-13, the Apostle Paul distinguished human wisdom from God's wisdom, human words from God's words. He wrote:

> For who among men knows the thoughts of a man except the spirit of the man which is in him? Even so the thoughts of God no one knows except the Spirit of God. Now we have received, not the spirit of the world, but the Spirit who is from God, so that we might know the things freely given to us by God, which things we also speak, not in words taught by human wisdom, but in those taught by the Spirit, combining spiritual thoughts with spiritual words.

He concludes this section (v. 14-16) by saying that "the natural man does not accept the things of God for they are foolishness to him . . . but we have the mind of Christ."

The Spirit alone, who is now within us, knows the mind of God. If we are going to pray prayers that God will answer, we're going to need to know what God is thinking so that we can pray according to his will.

We get some further light on this subject from Romans chapter 8:

> . . . the Spirit also helps us in our weakness; for we do not know how to pray as we should, but the Spirit Himself intercedes for us with groanings too deep for words; and He who searches the hearts knows what the mind of the Spirit is, because He intercedes for the saints (his holy ones—that's us) according to the will of God.
>
> ROMANS 8:26-27

Did you catch that? We don't know how to pray as we should?

But now Jesus lives in us. He is the mediator between God and man. He is our advocate before the Father and, as the Spirit, is actually praying inside of us. To have the mind of Christ and to know the will of God, we need to be in the Spirit as well. Ephesians 6:18 actually says, "Pray at all times in the Spirit."

That may seem like a tall order, but Jesus said that when the Helper came, he would guide us, teach us, and lead us into all truth.

Sometimes prayers will just come naturally. At other times, when you begin to pray and can't find the right words, a good starting place is this: "Jesus, I don't know how to pray. Teach me to pray. Put in my heart your prayers."

The Christian life is a journey. We don't go from being a kid learning long division to being the substitute teacher in a post-doctorate university physics class overnight.

As the Great Heart Specialist in this chapter said, "Peace I leave with you; My peace I give to you; not as the world gives do I give to you. Do not let your heart be troubled, nor let it be afraid."

That even includes fretting over how to pray. Just look to Jesus. Turn your heart to him. Keep it that simple. Having a conversation with him about anything you are concerned about is the best place to start.

DAY 52

JESUS, THE VINE

CHAPTER 15

If you had stood on the Mount of Olives at the time of Jesus and looked southwest toward Jerusalem, you would have seen a stunning sight: a beautiful temple built from huge limestone blocks, adorned with colonnades, gates, towers, and all sorts of elaborate golden design, glittering in the sun. The Temple consisted of a big open court, called the outer court, and within that, a structure called the Holy Place. That building housed many furnishings that played a part in the priests performing their sacred duties. Deep inside the Holy Place was another room, called the Holy of Holies. This was where the presence of God resided.

According to Josephus, at the entrance to the Holy Place hung a huge curtain some sixty feet long, thirty feet wide and about four inches thick (the width of a man's hand). Above the curtain was a golden vine with clusters of grapes the size of a man. Every time the priests entered that Holy Place to worship, offer prayers, and perform their duties, they saw this vine with its clusters of grapes above the entrance, beckoning them to enter into the presence of God.

The grape clusters evoked memories of the spies who went in to spy out the Promised Land and returned to Moses with huge clusters of grapes, indicative of the fruitfulness of the land.

There is also rich imagery in the Old Testament portraying Israel as God's vineyard: "For the vineyard of the Lord is the house of Israel2" (Isaiah 5:7). In Psalm 80:14-15, the writer was praying to God asking, "O God of hosts, turn again now, we beseech You; look down from heaven and see, and take care of this vine, even the shoot which Your right hand has planted . . ."

Symbols of grape vines were also engraved on ancient Jewish coins to remind Jews that they were God's vine, God's people.

You may wonder why God would compare his people in the Old Testament to a vine? The Prophet Ezekiel described the wood of the vine in Ezekiel 15:2-3: ". . . how is the wood of the vine better than any wood of a branch which is among the trees of the forest? Can wood be taken from it to make anything, or can men take a peg from it on which to hang any vessel?"

As I mentioned earlier, hardwood trees like mahogany, hickory, oak, and walnut are useful. They can be used to build cabinets, furniture, floors, veneer, gunstocks, and stairs—all sorts of items.

Vine wood, on the other hand, is useless. As Ezekiel said, you can't even use it to make a peg to hang a pot. A peg made of vine wouldn't hold even

---

2   The "house of Israel" referred to in Isaiah is a stand-in for the Jewish people. The original name for the people we call Jews today was the Hebrews, and was first used to describe Abraham (Genesis 13:13). They then became known as Israelites, the descendants from Abraham's grandson, Jacob, who God re-named "Israel." Jacob (Israel) had a son named Judah. Later still, from about the 6th century B.C. onward, they were known as Jews (Hebrew: "Yehudi"), which is a word derived from Judah.

your jacket. It is twisted, gnarled, and weak. The only thing a vine is good for is to produce fruit!

What a fitting wood God used to illustrate Israel! In themselves, they were not strong, beautiful, or useful. But as long as they remained humble and their hearts stayed soft and turned toward God, God could use them. They could bear fruit for God.

But they had failed. They had become proud. The result was no fruit—just an empty, worthless religion. Jesus was about to start all over again with the twelve, and upon that foundation, have a new people for himself that would bear fruit for God.

With that as a backdrop, let's return to the Last Supper.

Jesus had just finished speaking to his disciples' troubled hearts, telling them that he would leave them with his peace.

Now we come to chapter 15, where Jesus laid on them more mind-boggling truths that they still couldn't get their heads around. But they would understand eventually, once the Spirit came.

Jesus began by saying, "I am the true [the *real*] vine."

I can just imagine what must have been going through the minds of those disciples. I can see one of them, perhaps Thomas, shaking his head and thinking to himself, "Wait a minute. Stop! I thought Israel was God's vine."

This ran contrary to everything these men had grown up to believe.

In the Old Testament, Israel had one God and twelve tribes, and *they* were the vine. Not anymore!

What Jesus told the apostles must have given them momentary brain-freeze, like you get from drinking a cold drink too fast—another red-pill shocker.

Just like water, bread, air, lambs, and seeds were pictures to teach us and remind us of Jesus, here we see God's purpose for creating grapevines—to show us even more about who he is.

Jesus continued, "I'm the true [the *real*] vine, and my Father is the vinedresser."

Now it was God (the Father), who cared for the real vine, Jesus, and the twelve disciples as the branches. No longer would the people of God be defined by bloodlines or race. That picture was about to be put away. From this point on, God's real vine, Jesus, had come. Those connected to Jesus would be branches because they share in the same life as the vine.

The priests had to go inside the physical Temple, under the golden vine and grape clusters, and into the Holy of Holies in order to enter into the presence of God. But soon, once Jesus rose from the dead, the disciples would be able to enter into the presence of God and the *true* vine, without a priestly intermediary.

For three-and-a-half years, the disciples had been hanging out in the outer court of Jesus' ministry. Now he was leading them into the Holy of Holies.

FRUIT-BEARING

CHAPTER 15

> I am the true vine, and My Father is the vinedresser. Every
> branch in Me that does not bear fruit, He takes away; and
> every branch that bears fruit, He prunes it so that it may
> bear more fruit. You are already clean because of the word
> which I have spoken to you. Abide in Me and I in you. As
> the branch cannot bear fruit of itself unless it abides in
> the vine, so neither can you unless you abide in Me. I am
> the vine, you are the branches; he who abides in Me and I
> in him, he bears much fruit, for apart from Me you can do
> nothing.
>
> JOHN 15:1-5

Eight times in this chapter we see the word "fruit." In 15:16 Jesus said,
"You did not choose Me, but I chose you, and appointed you that you
would go out and bear fruit and that your fruit would remain." It's Jesus'
purpose for all of his disciples, including you and me, that we would bear
fruit and that our fruit would remain.

What is the fruit Jesus has in mind?

Let's think back to John 12, when Jesus told his disciples that if a grain of wheat falls into the earth and dies, it would then bear much fruit. The fruit he was speaking of was the fruit of *his* life, *his* character, reproduced in others.

Many take fruit bearing in John 15:16 to mean that we were all meant to be great evangelists who go out and win many people to the Lord. True, some are gifted with that calling—praise God. But many are not. Don't let your heart be troubled if you think you are not measuring up to what God is expecting of you, if you don't happen to be Billy Graham or some famous evangelist. The word "fruit" is rarely used in the New Testament in this way. Most often it is used in reference to the character of our lives.

Galatians 5:22 says, "But the fruit of the Spirit is love, joy, peace, patience, kindness, goodness, faithfulness, gentleness, and self-control."

Near the close of John chapter 13, before Peter interrupted Jesus with a question (that took the rest of the chapter and all of chapter 14 to answer), Jesus said, "A new commandment I give to you that you love one another, even as I have loved you, that you love one another. By this all men [all people] will know that you are My disciples, if you have love for one another" (John 13:34-35).

At the beginning of chapter 15, Jesus picked up again right where he had left off, telling them how they could do that. "Abide [remain] in Me and I in you and you will bear much fruit, for apart from Me, you can do nothing" (John 15:5).

Jesus then wrapped up his explanation about him being the vine and us being the branches by repeating his new commandment, not once, but twice: first in John 15:12-13, "This is My commandment that you love one another, just as I have loved you. Greater love has no one than this, that one lay down his life for his friends;" and then again in verse 17, "This I command you, that you love one another."

The Apostle Paul amplifies what love is in chapter 13 of his letter to the Corinthian believers. Love (or if you wish to substitute the word "Jesus") looks like this: "Love is patient, love is kind and is not jealous; love does not brag and is not arrogant, does not act unbecomingly; it does not seek its own, is not provoked, does not take into account a wrong suffered, does not rejoice in unrighteousness, but rejoices with the truth; bears all things, believes all things, hopes all things, endures all things. Love never fails."

(Warning: Forget trying to pull that off on your own. It's impossible. Only one person can love that way; that's Jesus.)

Jesus' heart was heavy that night as he left with them the most important instructions they needed to hear. Among the greatest things he wanted them to know was that they were to love one another, just as he had loved them. They would not be able to do that on their own, because apart from him they could do nothing. But if they would abide in him, they would produce the fruit of the Spirit and then love, and all of love's attributes, would be reflected in their characters and their relationships.

This was so very important to Jesus to communicate that we will find he was still not finished on this subject when we come to his final prayer to his Father in chapter 17, just before going to the cross.

DAY 54

PRUNING

CHAPTER 15

So far in chapter 15:

- Jesus is the vine
- We are the branches
- We are to abide in him
- And if we do, we will bear much fruit

Things were going good up until this point, but now we come to the more difficult part of this passage:

"If anyone does not abide in Me, he is thrown away as a branch and dries up; and they gather them, and cast them into the fire and they are burned" (John 15:6).

This may seem to get a little scary. But don't let your heart be troubled!

If you remember, back in John chapter 6 Jesus said, "All that the Father gives Me will come to Me, and the one who comes to Me I will certainly not cast out;" (v. 37) and "This is the will of Him who sent Me, that of all that He has given Me I lose nothing, but raise it up on the last day" (v. 39).

Based on the trustworthiness of Jesus' words, you need to ask yourself: If you have truly come to Jesus and you were a gift that the Father gave to him, will he cast you away? Is he not strong enough to keep you? Is it the will of his Father that you would be lost? The answer to all of these questions is "no."

If this is true, then what did Jesus mean when he said branches that did not abide in him would be thrown away and burned? What is he talking about?

This passage is not about whether or not a believer in Jesus can lose their salvation and be sent to hell, though some may interpret it this way. This whole passage is about bearing fruit. If you abide in Christ, you will bear fruit. If you are not abiding in Christ, you will need to be pruned so that you *will* bear fruit.

Imagine a grapevine emerging from the winter's cold. Suddenly, new growth and then blossoms begin to shoot out from the vine in every direction. For a short while, this can be a season of beauty. But the purpose for the vine is not just to produce wild branches. Its purpose is to bear fruit.

So, the caretaker of the vineyard must come and prune back the vine. Having much experience, he knows just where to cut. He will remove the excess new and tender branches and throw them in a pile where they will dry up. Then he will burn them because they are of no use.

Fruit is the manifestation of Christ in your life. If you are manifesting other kinds of fruit, you are not abiding in the vine, and those branches will need to be trimmed off.

Immediately before Paul listed the fruit of the Spirit in Galatians 5:22-23, he made another list called "the deeds of the flesh." Here is that list: "immorality, impurity, sensuality, idolatry, outbursts of anger, disputes, dissensions, factions, envying, drunkenness, carousing, and other things like these . . ."

After you became a Christian, did certain activities you once practiced or enjoyed doing seem to lose their attraction? Did they dry up? That was Jesus pruning inside of you, removing the useless branches that were not producing the kind of fruit he is looking for.

The sinful, self-destructive behaviors on Paul's list may have been manifest in your life prior to meeting Jesus. Some of them might still be hiding out, and may show up from time to time. Others may have been so much a part of you that they seem impossible to strip away and overcome.

But don't let your heart be troubled. God's patience goes far beyond our human patience. He is long suffering. God wants to transform you into the image of his Son. But this is not a project for which there is a short-term fix. For him to form you into his masterpiece will take time, and requires skill and attention to the smallest detail, in order to complete.

After coming to Jesus you will start to become aware of his high standards, his character, and the quality of life he lived. When you do, you may determine that to become more like him, you need to fix yourself.

But that's not your job—to fix or prune yourself. Nor is it any other person's job. That's God's job.

He is the one responsible for cultivating and pruning the vine. He will be working on that, utilizing the infinite variety of methods at his disposal, over the course of your lifetime, to produce *his* fruit in *your* life.

One verse in the middle of this section says, "If you abide in Me, and My words abide in you, ask whatever you wish, and it will be done for you" (John 15:7). I'm not positive on the correct interpretation for this verse, but if you look at the verse that precedes this one, the context seems to be those nasty branches that need to be taken away and burned up! Could it be that Jesus was telling us that as we abide in him, we would see those fruitless branches in our lives that need to go, and we will ask him to prune them away, and he will do it?

Regardless, one thing is for sure: The more you learn to abide in Jesus, the more fruitful you will become!

Oh, one last thing.

In the first 60 percent or so of chapter 15, Jesus talked to his disciples about fruit bearing. In the remainder of the chapter he pivoted and began to tell them to expect to be hated by the world.

Since a slave is not greater than his master and their master was hated and persecuted, then the disciples could expect the same.

What does this teach us? The more fruitful and the more like Jesus you become, the more, like him, you will be hated without a cause.

SADNESS & DESPAIR

CHAPTER 16

It had been one long, emotional, gut-wrenching evening for the disciples. They were hearing things from Jesus that were wonderful and amazing, but, knowing that he was really about to leave and face one of the most incomprehensible forms of death ever known to man, sadness had finally come to grip them. This whole drama, the physical life they had lived with Jesus, was about to come to an end.

Now we come to chapter 16. In this chapter, the disciples learned that they would be made outcasts from the synagogues; they would be killed; the people who killed them would think that by killing them they were offering service to God (v.2), but also that their oppressors would do these things because they didn't know the Father, or Jesus, so the disciples should not take it personally.

Jesus had not spoken like this to them from the beginning. It would not have been a very good recruiting tool. But they needed to hear it now, so that when it did happen, they would remember that he had told them so. But Jesus also acknowledged their deep sorrow and lovingly interjected a word of compassion. He could see the despair in their faces. He could sense it in the room. So he returned to something that he had said to them already, repeatedly, during the course of the evening—reinforcements were on the way. A cavalry was staged on the other side of the hill, awaiting the signal to charge in and deliver them from their sorrow. Once again, Jesus was talking to them about the Helper, the Holy Spirit.

Jesus also expanded upon the role the Holy Spirit would play when he did come, stating:

> And He, when He comes, will convict the world
> concerning sin and righteousness and judgment:
> concerning sin, because they do not believe in Me; and
> concerning righteousness, because I go to the Father and
> you no longer see Me; and concerning judgment, because
> the ruler of this world has been judged.
> JOHN 16:8-11

Let's paraphrase that:

- The Holy Spirit would convict people (pierce their consciences with awareness) about their sin. We can argue and debate and try to convince people that their life-styles and attitudes about Jesus are wrong, but only the Holy Spirit can convict them about personal sin.
- The Holy Spirit is the one who will make people aware of God's standard of righteousness, which can deliver them from self-righteousness, and lead them to discover righteousness from God that is not achievable outside of faith in Christ.
- The Holy Spirit will also enlighten them with the realization that there will be a day of judgment and the way they live has consequences. This will force them to make a decision to choose to follow Jesus or not. Satan will be totally judged and defeated at the cross. But will they go

on living his lie, or will they take the red pill for themselves that will deliver them from the power of sin and death and lead them to life?

Once again, Jesus could see that his disciples still were not getting what he was saying. They were still grappling to understand. So, once again, he addressed them with words aimed at comforting their troubled hearts. "Truly, truly I say to you, that you will weep and lament, but the world will rejoice; you will grieve, but your grief will be turned to joy" (John 16: 20). He reassured them once more that they would see him again, which would bring them great joy.

Chapter 16 ends with the disciples reaffirming their belief in Jesus, but Jesus countering that hopeful optimism by telling them that they were about to all be scattered and abandon him. This must have hit them like another crushing, ton of bricks.

Just like Jesus had personally encouraged and reassured Peter after telling him that he would deny him three times, he now reassures the whole group in the same way: "These things I have spoken to you, so that in Me you may have peace. In the world you have tribulation, but take courage: I have overcome the world" (John 16:33).

They could only see the immediate. Jesus was looking beyond to his resurrection and into eternity. He was not discouraged one bit, as they were, by what he saw!

There was a wonderful revelation contained in these words that the disciples still didn't get: "*In me*, you will have peace." There will always be tribulation, hardship, difficulties, uncertainties, confusion, and trouble in this world. But inside of every believer is a reservoir of peace—*his peace*—that can only be found as we abide *in* Jesus.

The other encouraging revelation, which the disciples would discover only later, is this: *Jesus* has overcome the world. Thoughts that they would be strong, they would stick with him until the end, and that they would never abandon him had to be dealt a deathblow. They could not overcome the world, but *Jesus* overcame the world. Only by relying on him and his strength could they overcome with him. This revelation for them would come—but only as a result of experiencing the cross.

On the other side of the cross they would discover *him* to be *the* over-comer. Only then would they realize that alone they could never have victory over sin, over weaknesses, and over troubled hearts. They would never be able to overcome the threat of persecution and death by trusting in themselves. There is only one way to experience overcoming strength and life. That is to abide in Jesus, the vine, for apart from him we can do nothing.

Jesus' Final Prayer with His Intimate Friends

CHAPTER 17

In the entire Bible there is no prayer like Jesus' prayer in John chapter 17. It stands alone. It takes less than four minutes to read aloud, but it will require the rest of eternity for us to comprehend. We're going to spend five coffee conversations talking about it, and we'll still just barely cover the basics.

If this prayer were a painting, it would make Leonardo da Vinci's "Mona Lisa" seem like a toddler's first attempts with a crayon. If it were a sculpture, it would make Michelangelo's statue of David look like an ordinary rock that hammer and chisel had yet to touch. If it were a score of music, it would make Handel's Messiah sound like a child banging on a piano.

There is nothing like it.

When we come to this incredible farewell prayer that Jesus prayed while with his disciples, we need to take off our shoes, because we are treading on holy ground.

Before we get into the prayer itself, I'd like to remind you of something very important. Studying the Bible just to gain information and knowledge will be of no benefit to you—just like it was of no benefit to the Pharisees. You need to come to this book with a humble heart and ask Jesus to reveal himself to you, just like he did to his disciples.

To get the most out of these next few coffee conversations, you should read Jesus' prayer first, before reading any of my comments.

The structure of this prayer is fairly simple. Jesus began addressing his Father by praying for himself. Then he prayed for his disciples. And finally, he closes by praying for believers of every age—including you and me.

Many Christians know this prayer as Jesus' "high priestly prayer." This is in reference to the high priests in the Old Testament who came into the holy presence of God to pray for the people and to make intercession on their behalf. In other places in the New Testament, particularly in the Book of Hebrews, Jesus is referred to as our High Priest.

In one of our earliest coffee conversations, I shared with you that the overall theme of the Bible is a love story. It is the story of Jesus and his quest to gain for himself a bride. Other themes include:

- Jesus is the Word, the expression of God, who came to reveal God to us
- Jesus is our Life
- Jesus is our Light
- Jesus is full of grace and truth (reality)
- Jesus is the real vine and we are the branches

All of these themes come together in this short, but remarkable, 650-word prayer.

In today's conversation, let's begin by focusing on the overall bridal theme. To review: from eternity past, the Father loved his Son so much that he wanted to give him a gift, an eternal companion that he could pour out his love upon, who would know him, and who would love him in return. That eternal companion would need to share the same life as her heavenly bridegroom.

Early in his prayer (John 17:2-3) Jesus prays, ". . . even as You gave Him authority over all flesh, that to all whom You have given Him [as a permanent gift], He may give eternal life. This is eternal life, that they may know You, the only true God, and Jesus Christ whom You have sent."

Here we see Jesus referring to the Father's gift—"all You have given Him." We see this again in verse 6: "I have manifested Your name to the men [and women] whom You gave Me out of the world; they were Yours and You gave them to Me . . ." And again in verse 24: "Father, I desire that they also, whom You have given Me, be with Me where I am."

In these opening lines of Jesus' prayer we also see mention of the theme that He (Jesus) came to "give eternal life" and that he was sent by the Father to become a man in order to take this bride from among those in the human race.

In addition, Jesus gives us the clearest definition of what eternal life is. Eternal life is not primarily related to time (eternal, in the sense that we will live forever, though we will). Eternal life is related to the quality or type of life Jesus came to give. He came to give us his life—*zoe* life—the very life that he and the Father had shared for all eternity. Praise God for that!

But Jesus even took it a step beyond that. His prayer reveals that we were not only given eternal life, but that "eternal life *is to know* the only true God, and Jesus whom he sent."

It is one thing to have that life, but it is another thing to know that life. It's like the difference between owning a car and having the experience of driving that car.

The Book of Genesis says, "Now the man [Adam] had relations with his wife Eve, and she conceived and gave birth," "Cain had relations with his wife and she conceived," and "Adam had relations with his wife again, and she bore a son and named him Seth" (Genesis 4:1, 17, 25).

The word behind the translation "had relations with" (to have sex with) is the Hebrew word *yada*, which means "to know." Literally, these verses should have been translated Adam and Cain "knew" their wives.

God created the man and the woman in the garden and said, "Be fruitful and multiply." God was all for sex (which should erase the concept that he is a prudish God). He created sex for men and women to enjoy. But he meant for it to be confined within the bounds of the husband-wife relationship. For a husband and a wife to have sex is to engage in the most intimate of human relationships possible, where they can express their love for one another freely, passionately, and completely.

In John 17:3 where Jesus prayed, "*that they may know You*, the only true God, and Jesus Christ whom You have sent," the Greek word there is *ginosko*, which can be and is used the same way as *yada* in Hebrew. Jesus did not pray that all those whom God had given him would know *about* him, or just know him intellectually, or know him from a distance. No! He prayed that they would know him in the deepest, most intimate, and experiential way possible. This is Jesus' heart desire *for you!!!* This is the way he wants you to know him *now,* not just in some future age to come.

God created the sexual relationship between a man and a woman to illustrate how intimate of a relationship he wants to have with you.

We also see in this prayer the theme that God's eternal purpose was to extend the divine family. Before the creation there was only God. He was alone. Then he created the man and the woman, which started the ball rolling for the entire human race to come into existence.

After the resurrection, Jesus began putting his life into those within the human race who believed in him, and the divine family began to expand. We see this in the portion of Jesus' prayer where he prays "that they may all be one, even as You Father, are in Me and I in You, that they also may be in Us" (v. 21).

Jesus came to earth and won a bride for himself out of his own creation. Then he brought her back, with him, into God. His motive was love.

Jesus concludes his prayer by reminding his Father that, "You sent Me, and loved them, even as You loved Me" (v. 23), "You loved Me before the foundation of the world" (v. 24), and that now "the love with which You loved Me may be in them [us], and I in them" (v. 26).

What a glorious insight we get into God's heart and eternal purpose in this prayer already!

OTHER THEMES FROM JOHN'S GOSPEL REFLECTED IN JESUS' PRAYER

CHAPTER 17

In our last conversation we covered the bridal theme and the eternal life that Jesus has given us as expressed in his priestly prayer. In order to have a bride, Jesus needed to impart his own life to those who would become his counterpart—his Mrs.—so that she would share the same form and quality of life that he possessed. He prayed that we would know him in the most intimate way possible, as portrayed by the most intimate of human relationships—the marriage union.

I also mentioned that this prayer touched on other themes that we have seen earlier as well:

- Jesus is the Word, the expression of God, who came to reveal God to us
- Jesus is our Light
- Jesus is full of grace and truth (reality)
- Jesus is the real vine and we are the branches

Let's look at those, one by one:

Jesus is the Word, the expression of God, who came to reveal the nature and heart of God to us.

- "The words which You gave Me I have given to them" (John 17:8)
- "I have given them Your word; and the world has hated them" (John 17:14).

Now we have that living Word inside of us. We can hear his voice. He has also left us with the written record of his words and the rest of the inspired, God-breathed Scriptures. Now we can be his instruments on earth to reveal his words, thoughts, and nature.

Jesus is our Light.

- "Now they have come *to know* that everything You have given Me is from You" (John 17:7, *emphasis mine.*)
- "They received [Your words] and *truly understood* that I came forth from You, *and believed* that You sent Me" (John 17:8, *empahsis mine*).

Through the revelation (light) given to us by the Holy Spirit, we have come to know and understand who Jesus is.

Jesus is full of grace and truth (reality).

- "Sanctify them [set them apart for the special use for which they were created] in Your truth; Your word is truth" (John 17:17).
- "For their sakes I sanctify Myself, that they themselves also may be sanctified in the truth" (John 17:19).
- "They are not of the world, even as I am not of the world" (John 17:16). Paraphrase: They are not of this world (the Matrix). Their

origin and destiny is another realm. They have been set apart to enjoy the reality of that other realm forever.

God's revelation to us comes as a result of his grace alone. His desire for us is that we be delivered from the kingdom of this world into the realm of knowing God as king and have an experiential knowledge of living in the reality of his kingdom. His prayer was that the Father would sanctify us (set us apart) from living a lie in an unreal world so that we could live in the truth.

Jesus is the real vine and we are the branches.

- "That they may all be one; even as You, Father, are in Me and I in You, that they also may be in us" (John 17:21).
- "I in them and You in Me, that they might be perfected in unity" (John 17:23).

These words echo the teaching Jesus had given earlier—probably within the hour—when he revealed himself to his disciples as the true vine. Through God's doing, we are in Christ and Christ is in us. As we abide in Jesus (the real vine) and he abides in us, we experience oneness with him and being one with every other believer.

There is so much more in this prayer. We haven't even begun to scratch the surface. In our next three conversations we'll be digging deeper into Jesus' prayer as well as what his current ministry in heaven is now.

DAY 58

JESUS' PRAYERS FOR YOU

CHAPTER 17

As Jesus prayed in the presence of his disciples, it was as if he had one foot planted on the earth and the other in eternity. He prayed with confidence and assurance, and as mediator between God and man, laid bare the deepest thoughts and intentions concerning God's eternal purpose and his plan for mankind that his disciples would ever hear. One new element that Jesus unveiled in this prayer concerned his glory.

In Old Testament times, after God instructed Moses to build the tabernacle, the glory of God came to reside inside of its innermost part, the Holy of Holies (Exodus 40:34-35). From the outside, this tabernacle (tent) did not appear glorious because it was covered over with ordinary brown animal (badger) skins.

Similarly, when Jesus came to earth, he took on the form of ordinary human flesh—nothing spectacular in appearance. From the outside, the human eye could not detect that the actual glory and presence of God dwelt within him, yet Jesus expressed the very nature of God. In the first chapter of John (v. 14 HCSB), John compared Jesus with the tabernacle: "The Word became flesh and took up residence among us. We observed

His glory, the glory as the One and Only Son from the Father, full of grace and truth." (The actual Greek word translated "took up residence" is "tabernacled.") In other words, Jesus became the living tabernacle among them.

In John 17, Jesus prayed that the Father would restore the glory that he had with the Father in his pre-incarnate state: "Now, Father, glorify Me together with Yourself, with the glory which I had with You before the foundation of the world" (John 17:5). Then he referred to the glory that the Father had given him in his current state of awareness: "I desire that they also, whom You have given Me, be with Me *where I am*, so that they may see My glory which You have given Me" (John 17:24). And by the end of his prayer, he revealed that he had *given them* the glory that the Father had given him (John 17:22, *emphasis mine*). The disciples began as those who beheld his glory, but were destined to become those who shared his glory. (The same is true of you and me!)

Mind-boggling. In one sense, as he was praying this prayer, he was preparing to leave. But in another sense, he was already gone.

At that moment, Jesus was already experiencing the reality of being in the eternal realm as he was bringing his requests for his disciples into the presence of his Father. From an eternal perspective, he knew that these prayers had already been answered. But as the disciples listened to these prayers, many of his words must have come across as very puzzling to them.

For instance: "The words which You gave Me I have given to them; and they received them and truly understood that I came forth from You" (John 17:8).

The disciples must have been thinking, *What? Wait a minute. We received your words and truly understood that you came forth from God? Based on our collective recollection, we hardly understood anything you were saying.*

You tell us that we're all going to scatter and abandon you, yet you believe that we will all be so tight, so united—just as you are with your Father— that this will cause the world to believe that the Father sent you? How can both of those things be true?

The glory the Father has given to you, you have given to us? What are you seeing? None of us can see or feel that. We're not looking very glorious right now.

The love that the Father has loved you with is going to be in us? At the same time, you are going to be in us? You must really know something we don't know, because right now, it is inconceivable to us how that is going to happen.

Inconceivable to them? Maybe. But not to Jesus. He knew that the Spirit, who was to be sent, would lead them into all truth.

Earlier he told them that they would weep and lament, but that their grief would be turned to joy. He didn't need to pray to the Father that the joy that was in him would be made full in his disciples. He already knew that was going to happen. Much of what Jesus prayed exuded thankfulness and confident declarations, more so than requests, as coming from one whose mission was accomplished and seemed to be primarily intended for his disciples to hear.

The substance of his prayer was simple, but profound:

- That we would intimately and experientially know him and know the Father (2-3)

- That the Father would keep us and protect us from evil and the evil one (11, 15)
- That the Father would sanctify us (set us apart) from living a lie to living in the truth (17, 19)
- That we would be one even as Jesus and the Father are one (11, 21, 23)
- That we would be with him where he is so that we could see his glory (24)

This was his heart for his disciples and for you then. This is still his heart for you now. What we learn from this prayer also gives us a hint as to what Jesus is doing in heaven right now, at this very minute!

We'll explore that next time.

JESUS' PRESENT MINISTRY

CHAPTER 17

In chapters 14 through 16 we learned that the Holy Spirit would be in us. Elsewhere, but specifically in the prayer from John chapter 17, we learned that:

- The Father is in the Son (verses 21, 23)
- The Son is in the Father (verse 21)
- We all are in the Father and in the Son (verse 21)
- The Son is in us (verses 23, 26)

Now that that is clearly understood (!), let's turn to the question, if Jesus is in us, what is he doing in us?

There are hints of what he is doing in his prayer from chapter 17, but other portions of the New Testament help us answer that question further.

The Book of Hebrews also tells us more about Jesus being our High Priest. It says that he will be a priest forever (Hebrews 7:21), and that he always lives to make intercession for us (Hebrews 7:25).

If one of the things he is doing for us now in the heavenly, unseen realm is interceding (praying) for us, what is he praying?

The answer is: the same things that he prayed for us in John 17:

- That we would intimately and experientially know him and know the Father
- That we would be kept and protected from evil and the evil one
- That we would be sanctified and set apart from living a lie to living in the truth
- That we would be one with all other believers even as Jesus and the Father are one
- That we would be with him where he is so that we could see his glory

One of the other precious themes in Jesus' prayer in John 17 that I'd like to spend some time on, and that has implications for our future security, was Jesus' assurance that the Father would keep us and protect us from evil and the evil one. Elsewhere in the New Testament we receive even more light on this.

There is a very short letter in the Bible written by a man named Jude. It's easy to find. It is one chapter long and it comes just before the last book in the Bible, the Book of Revelation.

Jude was the brother of James, and both men were half-brothers of Jesus. They were half-brothers because they shared the same mother—Mary—but Jesus' father was God, while James' and Jude's father was Joseph. Joseph and Mary had several other children after Jesus' miraculous conception and birth.

Each book of the Bible makes a special contribution to the whole, and Jude is no exception. If we were to take away any one book, we would miss one part of the overall revelation of God as he is presented in the Bible. Jude's notable contribution to our understanding is this: the keeping power of God.

Jude begins his short letter with, "Jude, a bondservant of Jesus Christ, and brother of James, to those who are called, beloved of God the Father, and *kept for Jesus Christ"* (*emphasis mine*).

Jude ends his letter with, "Now to Him who is able to *keep you* from stumbling, *and to make you stand in the presence of His glory blameless with great joy*, to the only God our Savior, through Jesus Christ our Lord, be glory, majesty, dominion and authority, before all time and now and forever. Amen!" (v. 24-25, *emphasis mine*).

Sound familiar?

Here we learn that we are kept *for Jesus Christ* so that we could be presented *to Jesus Christ.* Once again, we see the culmination of all history in view: the bride of Christ kept for Jesus, to be presented to him.

Jesus is doing other things in heaven besides praying for us right now. But John 17 reveals him to us as our great High Priest.

The prayers he is praying for us now have ramifications both today and in eternity. Once we die and go to be with him, we will continually marvel and wonder as the answers to the prayers he prayed then continue to unfold.

Praise God for such a High Priest.

Another insight we gain from Jesus' prayer is how we can more effectively pray for others. If you want to learn to pray for others according to God's will, then Jesus' prayers in John 17 would certainly be a model for you to follow.

The Apostle Paul was one who learned to pray for other believers according to the will of God. Two of his magnificent prayers are recorded in the

Book of Ephesians. The first is a prayer that the Ephesian believers would know Jesus:

> I . . . do not cease giving thanks for you, while making
> mention of you in my prayers; that the God of our Lord
> Jesus Christ, the Father of glory, may give you a spirit of
> wisdom and revelation in the knowledge of Him. I pray
> that the eyes of your heart may be enlightened so that you
> will know what is the hope of His calling [why he set you
> apart and all that he has to give you], what are the riches
> of the glory of His inheritance in the saints [that you
> will know all the riches of Christ that he has put in other
> believers as well], and what is the surpassing greatness of
> His power towards us who believe.
> EPHESIANS 1:16-19

Whew! In Paul's day it was not a grammatical faux pas to write in long, never-ending sentences. Bullet points had not become fashionable. In order to be faithful to the texts, most Bible translators wrote in long sentences as well, just to keep up with him!

The second marvelous prayer that reflects the heart of the Lord Jesus is found in Ephesians chapter 3:

> For this reason I bow my knees before the Father . . .
> that He would grant you, according to the riches of
> His glory, to be strengthened with power through His
> spirit in the inner man, so that Christ may dwell in your
> hearts through faith; and that you, being rooted and
> grounded in love, may be able to comprehend with all the
> saints what is the breadth and the length and height and

depth, and to know the love of Christ which surpasses
knowledge, that you may be filled up to all the fullness of
God.

EPHESIAN 3:14-19

Short version: Paul's earnest prayers for the Ephesians were 1) that God would give them revelation so that they would know Jesus Christ, and 2) that they would experientially know the love of Christ, and be filled with all the fullness of God.

All that we see in Paul's long, embellished prayers can be traced back to that single powerful prayer Jesus modeled for us in John chapter 17—that we would know God, and that we would know the love of God.

Through Jesus' model, you have now been given some of the greatest instructions for how to pray for yourself and for others according to the will of God!

THE IMPLICATIONS OF JESUS' PRAYER

As we conclude this study of John chapter 17, and as God gives us light, we will see more and more how fathomless Jesus' prayer really is. Resting on Jesus' assurance that his prayers would be answered, here are some of the conclusions that we can draw about the way Jesus sees us:

1. Jesus recognizes that the real, valid, legitimate life in you is no longer the fallen, sin-marred life that you inherited from Adam, but is now the same eternal, uncreated life that he and the Father share (v. 2).

2. Jesus sees you through the finished work that he accomplished on the cross: all sins completely forgiven—past, present, and future. And not only forgiven but forgotten, because he took them into the grave with him and left them there when he arose from the dead. He sees the power of sin broken as the result of the new life he has given you. He sees his victory as your victory, for he has overcome the world and the power of death (v. 4).

3. Jesus sees that the words the Father gave to him are now your words (v. 8). You have been given a new power of speech—words that are life-changing, up-building, encouraging, and empowering, and words that you can speak to others.

4. Jesus sees you as a believer. Faith is a gift from God that has been implanted in you so that you can believe that the things the Father has given to Jesus, Jesus has now given to you (v. 7-8).

5. Jesus sees you as being kept in him (v. 11-12). You are not held in his hand and then periodically dropped, depending on your feelings or experience. What he says of you is true, regardless of your doubt or shortcomings. When you stop believing what is true of you and lapse into believing a lie, resulting in behavior that does not match up with the new life he has given you, still you are secure and kept—not because of some teaching or some doctrine, nor because of your own efforts, but because God has placed you in Christ and He sees you *in Christ!*

6. Jesus sees you as one having access to the joy of God because *he* is in you (v. 13).

7. Jesus sees you as a person who is not of this world, just as he is not of this world (v. 14-16). This world, the Matrix, is not your home. You are in it, but not of it. You are just passing through. Your citizenship is in another realm—the realm where God lives and where Jesus lives, not the realm of shadows and pictures, but the realm behind those shadows and pictures where everything is real.

8. Jesus sees you with a new identity, as one who is exclusively set apart for him and him alone (v. 19).

9. Jesus sees you as part of the divine family. You are one (united) with all other believers as closely as Jesus is with the Father. And just as the Father is in Jesus and Jesus is in the Father and they are one, you are in them and one with them (v. 11 and 21).

10. Jesus sees you as already possessing the glory that he now has (fully expressing God—body, soul, and spirit), even though you have yet

to experience it all. Your future is not in doubt. You have already made it, though your eyes do not yet see it.

11. Jesus sees you as being loved by the Father just as much as the Father loves Jesus. How great a love is that! All things the Father has and is, he shares with Jesus, and all things they have and are, belong to you also. Since God is love, you were destined to meld into, be enveloped by, and know (experientially) the essence of love, just as it is known between the Father and the Son.

12. Jesus sees you already with him and with the Father in the realm that they have chosen to occupy and share with you so that you can experience their glory for all eternity (v. 24).

All of this we see in the seed form in Jesus' prayer, but it takes the rest of the New Testament to more fully explain, unfold, and develop these revelations.

I'll give you just two short examples taken from the Apostle Paul's writings:

Paul began his first letter to a group of Christians living in the Greek city of Corinth with this salutation: "Paul . . . to the church of God which is at Corinth, to those who have been sanctified in Christ Jesus, saints by calling, with all who in every place call on the name of our Lord Jesus Christ, their Lord and ours" (1 Corinthians 1-2).

Here he addressed them as those who were already sanctified (set apart for God) and who were "saints by calling." "Saints" is just another word for "holy ones."

In Paul's eyes (and in God's eyes) that is what they were. (And that is what *you* are!) Yet as you read his letter to the Corinthians, you'll find that they still had all sorts of problems. They were still babies in their spiritual understanding of the truth:

1. There were divisions among them.
2. They were jealous of one another.
3. There was immorality among them.
4. They were suing one another.
5. Some were still worshipping idols (maybe not bowing down to stone statues, but worshipping counterfeit and deceitful "gods" such as money, fame, knowledge, pleasure, power, false religious practices, or seeking to derive worth from those foolish and deceptive earthly things).

Those Corinthian believers had many problems. Experientially, they were not perfect. They were still here on the earth and working these things out. But their experience did not override the truth. God never stopped seeing them in Christ, as saints, as holy ones. His Spirit was still in them. He was still loving them—correcting and pruning them, giving them light and revelation. His goal remained unchanged: to bring them to spiritual maturity so that they would see themselves as he saw them.

The second example comes from Paul's letter to the Romans. There he writes,

> And we know that God causes all things to work together
> for good to those who love God, to those who are called
> according to His purpose. For those whom He foreknew,
> He also predestined to become conformed to the image
> of His Son . . . and these whom He predestined, He also
> called; and these whom He called, He also justified; and
> these whom He justified, He also glorified.
>
> ROMANS 8:28-30

To paraphrase, God causes all things to work together for those who love God and are called according to his eternal purpose (to be his loving bride). He knew who you were before the world ever existed. He had already predetermined that you would be conformed to the image of Jesus, his Son. In time and space he called you to himself and saved you. He justified you, removing the guilt and penalty of your sin instantaneously, once you received Christ, and pronounced you righteous and holy in him. Finally, though you don't see it or haven't experienced it yet, you have already been glorified.

Then he goes on to say,

> For I am convinced that neither death, nor life, nor
> angels, nor principalities, nor things present, nor things
> to come, nor powers, nor height, nor depth, nor any other
> created thing, will be able to separate us from the love of
> God, which is in Christ Jesus our Lord.
> ROMANS 8: 38-39

Do you see the theological connections between what Paul wrote and Jesus' prayer in John 17? We need the gospels to see what God, coming in the flesh, looks like and what he accomplished on the cross. But we also need the rest of the inspired New Testament writings to help us understand and interpret the full revelation of who Jesus is, what his purpose is, and who we are in him.

To summarize, once more:

» God sees you in Christ.

» Jesus' history is your history.

» Jesus' future is your future.

» Jesus' glory is your glory.

» Jesus' words are your words.

» Jesus' life is your life.

» Jesus' authority is your authority.

» Jesus' knowledge of the Father has become your knowledge of the Father.

» Jesus' love for the Father and the Father's love for Jesus is your love for the Father and your love for Jesus.

» Jesus' union with the Father and the Father's union with Jesus is your union with the Father and your union with Jesus.

» This is who you are in the realm of the Spirit and in the eyes of God. God is truth; God is what is real. Outside of God are only the lies and deceit we have experienced while living inside the Matrix.

GETHSEMANE

CHAPTER 18

Consider for a moment the content, the assurance, and the loftiness of Jesus' prayer in John chapter 17. These prayers were prayed only hours before he would be hung on a cross and crucified. If you read the Book of John alone, you might conclude this was the last earthly prayer that Jesus ever prayed, but it was not.

Chapter 18, verse 1 begins, "When Jesus had spoken these words [the prayer of John 17], He went forth with His disciples over the ravine of the Kidron [on a bridge spanning the Kidron Valley that connected Jerusalem to the Mount of Olives], where there was a garden, into which He entered with his disciples." From there John goes on to describe Jesus' betrayal and arrest. What he doesn't include is that in this garden (the Garden of Gethsemane) Jesus prayed another prayer, his final recorded prayer *before* his arrest.

You'll find detailed accounts of this in Luke 22:39-46, Mark 14:32-42, and Matthew 26:36-46.

I don't know why John omitted this significant event in Jesus' life. At

Gethsemane, Jesus' prayer was so intense that it caused him to sweat drops of blood! This is nothing like the prayer we read in John 17. Jesus' Gethsemane prayer was different. Jesus' Gethsemane prayer centered on whether or not there was any other way that he could fulfill the plan of God apart from going to the cross.

The conclusion was that no, there was not. The matter was settled with those famous words, "Not my will, but Your will be done."

The agony and tears of those prayers in the garden were not primarily over the fact that he was about to experience one of the most brutal forms of execution imaginable—he had known this day was coming since childhood. What caused his soul such anguish and despair was knowing that he was about to experience something so dark, so incomprehensively devastating, that it would be almost impossible to bear. For all eternity Jesus had enjoyed perfect, unbroken communion with his Father. They shared the same life. Divine love flowed between them. But this was about to be taken from him. He knew he was going to be abandoned by his Father. He was about to experience, for the first time ever, separation from God, as the wrath of God was poured out upon him as the penalty for all the sins of the world, which he bore on our behalf.

Two thoughts come to mind as to why John may have omitted the story of Gethsemane. First, his stated reason for why he wrote his gospel was: "These things have been written so that you may believe that Jesus is the Christ, the Son of God; and that believing you may have life in his name" (John 20:31). With so much evidence and proofs already presented in this book, John must not have been inspired to think it necessary to include this story in order for people to believe.

The second possible reason is that in the high-priestly prayer of John 17, we see a triumphant Jesus. There were no doubts, concerns, or anguish expressed in that prayer. As he prayed to his Father in the upper room, we see no wavering whatsoever on how things would turn out. In his mind, the cross was already a thing of the past: "I have glorified You on the earth, *having accomplished the work* which You have given Me to do" (John 17:4).

Jesus had not yet gone to Gethsemane, or to the cross, where he performed his redemptive work. Yet in his mind, the work God had given him to do was already finished. In fact, there was tremendous joy in his heart as he prayed this prayer: "But now I come to You [Father]; and these things I speak in the world so that they may have My joy made full in themselves" (John 17:13).

The cross was part of the eternal plan of God, conceived before the creation of the world. In the mind of Jesus and in the mind of God, this plan had already been executed and flawlessly completed even before it happened in real time and space in 30 A.D. Jesus was assured, as he prayed, that this plan would not fail. Thus, the last prayer of Jesus that John records in his gospel was the one in chapter 17. That was all that John must have felt was necessary for us to see.

JESUS' ARREST & TRIAL

CHAPTER 18

Coming down from the theological clouds of John chapter 17, followed by his agonizing prayers in the Garden of Gethsemane, we're now back to the action of Jesus' final hours.

Chapter 18 briefly describes Judas' betrayal, Jesus' trial before the religious leaders, and his interrogation by the Roman governor of Judea, Pontius Pilate. These events get more attention in the other gospels, but we'll take a brief look at how things went down.

Following their meal together in the upper room and Jesus' high-priestly prayer, he led his disciples to the Garden of Gethsemane. They probably arrived at the garden somewhere around nine in the evening. This was normally a peaceful place, more of an orchard than a garden, where Jesus and his disciples frequently met together. (There are olive trees standing there today that are more than 2,000 years old, dating back to the time of Jesus.) Gethsemane means "oil press," and it was home to a notable oil press where olives were crushed to make oil.

Judas had betrayed Jesus to the religious leaders, receiving thirty pieces of silver in exchange for identifying him to the Roman soldiers so that they could arrest him. But for a few hours, while his disciples slept and Jesus prayed in the Garden, all was quiet.

Then, sometime close to midnight, Judas arrived, accompanied by a battalion of men (a cohort), consisting of 600 soldiers carrying torches and lanterns. There were also some Jewish Temple guards, along with some of the chief priests and Pharisees. They arrested Jesus without any resistance on his part.

But Peter, the disciple whom Jesus said would betray him three times, was not ready for Jesus to be arrested without a fight.

Though they all must have been scared, I have to give credit to Peter for his courage. Jesus and the disciples were outnumbered sixty-to-one. Still, Peter pulled out a small sword, which he had concealed under his garment, and took a swing at Malchus, the servant of the high priest.

He wanted to split Malchus's head open like a melon, but he was trained as a fisherman, not a warrior. He missed his mark and ended up only lopping off Malchus's ear. Jesus intervened and touched the bloody side of Malchus's head, and his ear was instantaneously restored. He told Peter to put away his sword. Jesus' kingdom was of another world; Peter and the other disciples were not there to fight.

And so the soldiers and guards seized Jesus and hauled him away. The eleven remaining disciples fled in fear.

A number of trials and inquiries took place during the night and early morning. Jesus appeared before Annas, and then Caiaphas, the High Priest. (Annas was actually the father-in-law of Caiaphas and the patriarch among the high priests. He was on duty as a backup, in case something went wrong and Caiaphas couldn't carry out his duties.) Once Caiaphas had interrogated him, he hastily arranged for an emergency meeting of the Sanhedrin, the supreme council of the Jewish people, consisting of seventy-one men—a third from the Pharisees, a third from the Sadducees, and a third from the elders.

When it was safe, Peter and John followed the crowd that had taken Jesus from a distance, to see what would happen to him. Because John (referred to in the text as "another disciple") knew the high priest, he entered into the courtyard next to the high priest's residence. Peter had to remain outside. But John spoke to the doorkeeper, a slave girl, and persuaded her to let Peter in.

The slave girl recognized Peter and asked him if he was one of Jesus' disciples. But Peter denied it. Twice more he was questioned regarding his association with Jesus, and twice more he denied it. Immediately after the third time, a rooster crowed, just as Jesus had predicted it would.

Meanwhile, Jesus was interrogated, falsely accused, and beaten. Yet his demeanor in front of Annas, Caiaphas, and later before Pontius Pilate, was regal, fulfilling a prophecy from Isaiah 53:7 that said, "He was oppressed and he was afflicted, yet he did not open his mouth. Like a lamb that is led to slaughter, and like a sheep that is silent before its shearers, so he did not open his mouth."

The Jews wanted to see Jesus put to death, but in life and death matters, they needed to get permission from the Roman authority. So they sent him over to Pilate, the Roman governor, who had jurisdiction over Jerusalem. By then, it was about six or seven in the morning.

The Jews found Jesus guilty of blasphemy, but that wouldn't fly with Pilate. He would have told them that this was a religious matter they needed to deal with on their own. So instead, they accused him of claiming to be a king—which was high treason to Rome, punishable by execution.

This news frightened Pilate. If word got back to the Emperor in Rome that Pilate had let a man off who was challenging Rome's authority, it would have brought Pilate's career to an abrupt and unpleasant end. But Pilate was conflicted because did not think that Jesus was guilty of any crime.

He asked Jesus, "So you are a king?"

Jesus replied, "You say correctly that I am a king. For this I have been born, and for this I have come into the world, to testify to the truth [to what is real]. Everyone who is of the truth hears My voice."

Pilate was puzzled. "What is truth [what is reality]?"

Jesus didn't answer.

If he had answered, his answer would have probably gone something like this: "*I am* the reality. *I am* the Red Pill!"

DAY 63

BARABBAS

CHAPTER 19

It was the governor's custom to release one prisoner each year during the Passover celebration. Pilate thought he could get Jesus off by offering the people a choice of releasing either him or a notorious criminal named Barabbas. *Surely,* Pilate thought, *the crowd won't choose Barabbas.* But the chief priest and Jewish leaders began inciting the raucous crowd until they shouted out in unison, "Kill Jesus. Release Barabbas!"

Who was this Barabbas character? His identity reveals even more of God's pre-ordained and sovereign plan.

To some, Barabbas was a revolutionary hero. To others, he was nothing more than a run-of-the-mill, no-good, dead-ender. He was in prison for a murder he had committed during an insurrection against the government in Jerusalem. But there was one other fascinating thing about him. That was his name.

You see, his full name was Jesus Barabbas. Barabbas means "Son of the Father." So his name literally meant, "Jesus, Son of the Father!" Just as different sacrifices and feasts were pictures to help us understand who Jesus was, so you will see another amazing picture in the person of Barabbas. God was still in the business of painting pictures to help us understand his plan right up until the end. We see this picture enacted on the Day of Atonement.

The Day of Atonement was a very special day for the Jews. It was the only day each year when the high priest was allowed to go inside the Holy of Holies to sprinkle blood from a sacrifice before the presence of God to cover over the sins of the people. On that day, two identical goats are brought to the Temple. In appearance, there was to be no difference between the goats at all. The high priest would draw two lots from an urn, called the *calpi*.

The lots were identical, except that the inscription on one read, "For Jehovah" and the other read, "la-Azazel," meaning "For the Evil One." The high priest held a lot over the head of each goat. The goat that drew the lot "For Jehovah" was killed. It was sacrificed on the altar, its blood was sprinkled in the Holy of Holies, and its carcass was taken to an outer altar, farther up on the Mount of Olives, and burned to ashes.

The goat that drew the lot "la-Azazel" was turned to face the people. The high priest then laid his hands on the head of this goat and prayed over it, symbolically placing on it all the sins of the people for the entire past year. Then he faced the people and solemnly pronounced to them, "You shall be cleansed!"

This goat, known as the scapegoat (you've heard that word, haven't you?) was then led out of the Temple and across the bridge to the Mount of Olives. There it was handed over to a Gentile, a non-Jew, and led away into the wilderness, where it was allowed to go free, but where it eventually died.

Are you beginning to see the picture here?

Barabbas and Jesus outwardly had the same names and titles. Jesus was pictured in both parts of this sacrifice. On one hand he was the pure and righteous one who died to forgive us of our sins to make us righteous before God (the "For Jehovah" goat). On one other hand, he also was the one who bore all of our sins and carried them away (the "la-Azazel" goat) so that we could be set free.

And, when the Jews turned Jesus over to Pilate, that fulfilled the illustration that the scapegoat would be turned over to a Gentile who was given the authority to take it away to death. Our God knew exactly what he was doing and planned everything down to the last detail.

So the people selected Barabbas, representing the scapegoat, as the one to be set free. The real "Son of the Father"—Jesus—would be executed.

Pilate then ordered Jesus to be "scourged." From information we gather from the other gospels, as well as from actual historical accounts and what medical experts say regarding the effects of scourging on the human body, the punishment Jesus endured was even more graphic than this word implies.

The Roman soldiers seized Jesus and stripped him of his clothes. They tied his hands and tethered him to a stake in front of the Fortress of Antonia, next to the Temple, where the Roman army was garrisoned. Then they administered a brutal whipping—thirty-nine lashes—with a small whip made of nine braided leather thongs, studded with sharp pieces of bone, spikes, and rock that ripped into the flesh on his shoulders, back, chest, and the back of his legs, producing 351 separate lacerations. Flesh and muscle were ripped away from his bones; later, as he hung on the tree, David's prophecies from the twenty-second Psalm concerning the Messiah were fulfilled: "I can count all my bones. They look, they stare at me."

When they finished the whipping, the soldiers hastily draped Jesus' clothes over his bloody body and dragged him back into the fortress where they taunted, mocked, and beat him some more. They removed his clothes and placed a purple robe on him, as if dressing him in the robes of a king. One soldier ripped off several branches from a thorny bush growing inside the fortress courtyard. He wove them together into a crown and drove it into Jesus's head. Another soldier placed a stick in his hand as a scepter. They mocked him and bowed down to him, as if he were a king.

It took real cowards to do that to one who had already gone through a previous beating and then been nearly whipped to death. When they finally tired of mocking and beating him, they removed the purple robe and dressed him in his own clothes again. Then they led him out to be crucified.

DAY 64

THE CRUCIFIXION

CHAPTER 19

Jesus' crucifixion and burial are described in chapter 19. By now, it was probably around 8 a.m. on Friday morning, a mere twelve hours since Jesus' priestly prayer in the upper room, but years away in tone. Pilate ordered six hundred of his soldiers to go before Jesus and the other two criminals who had also been sentenced, commanding them to line the road leading to the place of execution and control the crowd. Remember, Jews from all over the Empire were gathered in Jerusalem to celebrate the Passover, and worshipers had already begun streaming down the mountain toward the Temple with their lambs to have them slaughtered for the Passover Feast that night. An estimated twenty thousand lambs met their fate that day.

Each of the three men sentenced to die was required to carry his own *patibulum,* or crossbeam, to which he would be nailed. Each patibulum was about six feet long, five inches thick, and ten inches high, weighing about forty pounds. Shouldering the beam on his fresh wounds, Jesus staggered forward up the hill.

At one point, Jesus stumbled and fell, sprawling on the ground in front of an onlooker—a black man from the city of Cyrene on the coast of North Africa named Simeon. One of the guards ordered Simeon to pick up Jesus' patibulum and carry it the rest of the way for him.

It was about 9 a.m. when the soldiers arrived at the site of execution. They stripped Jesus and the other criminals naked, and the four soldiers who had guarded Jesus on the way up the mountain divided his garments among themselves.

Jesus had been wearing a tunic (or robe), woven in a single piece (John 19:23). Innocent sounding, perhaps. But first-century Jews, familiar with Jewish tradition, would have understood the meaning of this seamless robe. They would have known from Exodus 28 and 39 that it was the High Priest who was commanded to wear a seamless robe. Subtly but symbolically, Jesus had donned the attire of a High Priest when he went to the cross to atone for the sin of the entire world.

Since his robe was seamless and therefore valuable, the soldiers threw dice for it. King David, in Psalm 22, foretold this as well: "They divide my garments among them, and for my clothing they cast lots." Another prophecy fulfilled.

Simeon placed Jesus's patibulum on the ground. Jesus was then shoved down, rolled onto his back in the dust, and stretched out his arms to receive the nails.

The soldiers drove seven-inch-long, tapered iron spikes through his wrists. The pain must have been excruciating. Once he was fastened to the crossbeam, they hoisted him up and affixed the patibulum to a large tree. Then they drove another nail into his feet, fastening them to the tree trunk. The weight from his own body, suspended on the patibulum, caused his shoulders to be immediately dislocated. This fulfilled another messianic prophecy from Psalm 22: "And all my bones are out of joint."

Contrary to paintings and images we see of Jesus and the other criminals nailed to three separate crosses (poles stuck in the ground with crossbeams), John 19:21 says that their bodies (plural) would not remain on *the* cross (singular). Most likely, this means that the soldiers secured the other two criminals to the same tree—a living tree—one on Jesus's right and one on his left. This would correspond to what was written in Deuteronomy 21:23 and Galatians 3:13, "Cursed is anyone who hangs on a tree."

The prisoners' crimes were written on signboards and nailed above each of their heads. The signboard above Jesus' head read, "Jesus the Nazarene, the King of the Jews." Pilate himself had ordered it. It was written in three languages—Hebrew, Latin, and Greek—for all to read. The chief priests disputed with Pilate. They wanted it to read something else. But Pilate would not back down. According to him, the only thing that he could find Jesus guilty of was that he truly was king of the Jews.

Death by crucifixion is slow and agonizing. Whoever invented this insidious punishment had a sick and sadistic mind. From the moment victims were suspended on the tree, the pressure on their chests made breathing extremely difficult. They must push up on their feet to relax their chest muscles long enough for them to exhale. Then they fall back down, gasping for air. This agonizing process continues until the dying man has no more strength and is too exhausted to push up anymore. Add to that the muscle cramps, the flies landing on open wounds that cannot be swatted, the sweat that cannot be wiped from the eyes—it must be the most gruesome of all deaths.

Jesus took pity on his mother at the very end. He looked in her direction and saw Mary standing next to John. Knowing her heart was being ripped apart, he addressed her first and told her that, from then on, John would be her son. Then he looked at John and told John to take care of Mary as if she were his own mother. Those were the last words he spoke to another human being that day.

Jesus hung on that tree from 9 a.m. until noon. At that point, darkness fell over the land. That was when the Father turned his face away from his Son and withdrew his presence. Jesus was abandoned. For the next three hours Jesus hung on that tree, bearing in his body all of the sin of the whole world. The Scriptures teach that since the fall of Adam, the wages of sin have been death. Jesus became sin for us. Therefore, he had to die.

There on the cross, Jesus took upon himself the wrath of God for all the individual sins ever committed—for every murder, every rape, all harm ever inflicted on one person by another, and every lie. He bore the punishment for it all.

In addition to all the individual sins, he took into himself the very sin-infected nature of the human race. As the serpent in the wilderness was lifted up on the pole, so Jesus was lifted up on the cross and became sin for us. Praise God, that now those of us who have been infected with sin can look to Jesus and live!

Everything negative in the created universe was placed on Jesus, on the cross, that day. The last enemy was death itself. That too was placed on him and taken into the grave.

A little before 3 p.m., he stirred. Mustering all the strength he had left, he raised his head toward heaven and cried out in a loud voice, "My God, my God, why have You forsaken Me?" Then with another loud cry he shouted, "It is finished!" He bowed his head and uttered his final words, "Father, into Your hands I commit My spirit." And then he breathed his last breath.

We learn from the other gospels that at that very moment, the earth shook. Stones split apart, and the veil of the Temple was torn in two from top to bottom. When the centurion who was overseeing the execution saw all these things, he became terrified and exclaimed, "Truly this man was the Son of God!"

DAY 65

BURIAL

CHAPTER 19

The Jewish leaders were anxious to hasten this ordeal and get it over with as soon as possible. Sundown was approaching, and the Sabbath was just a few hours away. Jewish law required the burial of criminals on the same day as their execution. The Romans were much less humane. They often left the corpses of dead bodies hanging on trees for days until the birds and rats ate all the flesh away.

The Jews got permission from Pilate to have the criminals' legs broken so they would die faster and could be taken away. The soldiers took clubs and started breaking the legs of the victims just below the knees. This would prevent them from pushing off against the tree trunk in order to exhale. Suffocation would then occur within a matter of minutes. The soldiers made their way around the tree, breaking the leg bones of the first criminal and then the second. But when they came to Jesus, they saw that he was not breathing. He was obviously already dead.

Jesus, the *real* Passover Lamb, fulfilled the picture God gave at the first Passover when the Jewish people made their exodus from Egypt. There God instructed Moses and Aaron that none of the bones of the lambs should be broken (Exodus 12:46). This was also confirmed by another prophecy from Psalm 34:20 that said, "He keeps all his bones, not one of them is broken."

Just to be sure that Jesus was dead, one of the soldiers thrust a spear between his ribs, puncturing his heart. Blood and water flowed from his side. This fulfilled another prophecy: "They shall look on him whom they pierced." This was no small wound. It was large enough that after the resurrection, Thomas could fit his hand inside of it.

When it was all over, and all three victims were dead, the crowd dispersed. The soldiers went back to the fortress. The Jewish leaders returned to their homes. The out-of-town visitors departed for the houses where they were being hosted or to one of the countless temporary shelters that peppered the Mount of Olives and the surrounding hillsides during the festivals. The remaining local inhabitants went back to their residences.

Some of the women who had been following Jesus lingered behind to see what would become of his body, but eventually they too returned to the city and began preparing spices for his burial.

After the crucifixion, Joseph of Arimathea went to Pilate and asked for the body. Once Pilate confirmed that Jesus was dead, he granted permission for Joseph to take it. Joseph took Jesus's body down from the tree and carried it away to a tomb that he had purchased to use for his own burial. Nicodemus, the religious man who had come to Jesus during the night and questioned him about the kingdom of God, brought about seventy-five pounds of spices—myrrh and aloes—mixed with perfumes (Luke 23:56) that the women had prepared, and, together, he and Joseph wrapped the body in an eight-foot linen cloth. The two men sprinkled the sweet-smelling mixture between the folds of the shroud and hastily finished their work between the hours of 4 and 6 p.m., just before the Sabbath began.

The tomb was a subterranean cave, carved out of limestone rock. It had two chambers—a larger, square entry room for use as a mourning chamber where people could gather, and a smaller, rectangular alcove cut out of the wall, where the body was laid. Once Jesus' body was in place, Joseph and Nicodemus dislodged a large stone that was perched in an elevated position in front of the entryway, and it rolled down the slight incline and came to rest, sealing the cave.

Throughout Jerusalem that night there were those who joyfully celebrated the Passover Feast. Others, more subdued, pondered the day's events as they ate. And then there were those who had loved Jesus, who had no stomach for the meal at all. They were confused, crushed, lost, and brokenhearted.

The Resurrection

CHAPTER 20

Chapter 20 describes the resurrection. This was a big day—Sunday morning, the first day of the week.

In Genesis, when God created the heavens and the earth, he worked for six days, and then on the seventh day he rested. The Jewish calendar designates Saturday as the day of rest. Therefore, Sunday, naturally, would be the first day of the new week.

Jesus had predicted in John chapter 2 that three days after he was killed he would rise again. For the Jews, any part of a day counts as a full day. Jesus was crucified on a Friday. That is one day. Then there was Saturday, the Sabbath. That makes two days. Then he rose on Sunday morning. That accounts for three days.

Early that morning, Mary Magdalene came to the tomb and saw the stone in front of the entrance rolled away. Mary was a popular name in Jesus' day. There are several Marys' listed in the New Testament: Mary, the mother of Jesus; Mary of Bethany, Lazarus' sister; this Mary—Mary Magdalene; and others.

Mary Magdalene was a follower of Jesus who loved him dearly. She was from a fishing town on the Sea of Galilee called Magdala. She is mentioned a dozen or more times in the gospels, more frequently than most of the apostles. She is known for having Jesus cast seven demons out of her. She must also have been a wealthy woman because Luke mentioned that she was one of the women who traveled with Jesus and his twelve apostles, helping support them financially as they traveled.

She (a woman!) is also honored as the first evangelist in the New Testament, having been the first to see Jesus resurrected from the dead and then return to announce to the apostles, "I have seen the Lord!"

Despite all that Jesus had taught them, up until this point none of the disciples, including Mary, had understood the Scriptures that Jesus must rise from the dead (John 20:9).

Several things stand out as we read this chapter, but I'll only touch on a few.

When Mary first saw Jesus, she thought that he was the gardener. She didn't recognize him. She asked him where he might have taken Jesus' body. But then Jesus spoke to her in that endearing way which she was used to hearing when he called her name: "Mary!" It was then that she recognized who he was.

This is classic Jesus, and a lesson we cannot overlearn: even in his resurrection, it takes Jesus to reveal Jesus, God to reveal God. Everything we learn and know about him comes from revelation.

Mary was so overwhelmed that her immediate response was to breach all male-female protocols of the day and cling to him, as if she would never let him go. Then Jesus said to her, "Stop clinging to Me, for I have not yet ascended to the Father; but go to My brothers and sisters and say to them, I ascend to My Father and your Father, and My God and your God" (John 20:17).

This is such an amazing statement on so many levels!

The creator, the God-man Jesus, calling us his brothers and sisters! Elsewhere, in Hebrews 2:11, we read that Jesus is not ashamed to call us his brothers and sisters.

What does it mean to not be ashamed? That's just another way of saying, "I have no reservations whatsoever; in fact, I am so proud to call people like you my brother or my sister."

God's brothers! God's sisters! That's what we are. We've been accepted and made part of the divine family. God the Father—my Father, your Father—just like he is Jesus' Father! Truly amazing! Incomprehensible! It is all because we now share the same life! And as more people come to know Jesus, that family gets bigger and bigger by the day.

Another thing that makes the fact that God is our Father and we are his family so amazing is that it was the eternal purpose of the infinite God to become a man. Becoming a man was not just some sideshow or temporary necessity. Don't think that by Jesus assuming a physical body to die on the cross for us that he would then return to heaven to be just like he was before. No!

Do you realize that God once and forever altered who he was by becoming a man, a human being? This is the way he will remain forever and ever.

Right now, in heavenly, unseen realms, in that alternate reality that we have been learning about, there is a man with a physical body who rules the entire universe. He will never change. He will remain the same in the new heaven and earth, awaiting us in the age to come. Our God is not some alien creature that we will never really be able to relate to. Our God is a man!

Praise God for his resurrection! Praise God that we can know him now in Spirit because he has now come to live inside of us. And praise God that not only will we know him in eternity as the Spirit who lives within us, but we will also be able to see him, touch him, and know him as a human in his new body—all while we are in our new bodies, which we also will receive.

Too wonderful! What a God we have!

DAY 67

BREAKFAST ON THE BEACH

CHAPTER 21

We've now come to chapter 21, the last chapter in the Book of John. Following his resurrection, during the next forty days, Jesus appeared to his disciples a number of times before finally ascending to his Father. This last chapter of John describes one of those occasions.

This particular appearance took place at the Sea of Tiberias (also known as the Sea of Galilee). Seven of the disciples had decided to go fishing together. They pushed out from shore in the afternoon and fished all night, but caught nothing. At daybreak, as they were returning in the boat, they heard someone yell from the shore, "Cast the net on the right-hand side of the boat and you will find a catch."

They did and came up with such a large catch (153 fish, to be exact) that it almost broke their net.

John, whose self-description was "the disciple whom Jesus loved," said to Peter, "It is the Lord!"

Peter was stripped down to his underwear for work, but he hastily threw on his outward garment, dove in the water, and began free-styling it for shore at a rapid clip.

Jesus had some fish, along with some bread, already warming on a charcoal fire. He invited the men to join him for breakfast.

As with everything he did, there was no missed opportunity with Jesus. This encounter had a purpose.

Though Peter had received the Holy Spirit, he was still broken and carried a wound of guilt. He was not yet ready to be the apostle, the spokesman for the church, and the "fisher of men" that Jesus had called him to be. Though Peter was so excited to see Jesus, he was still not completely secure being with Jesus, as a friend should be. The guilt of his betrayal must have been chillingly re-activated the moment he saw that charcoal fire.

The words "charcoal fire" appear together only twice in the whole Bible—both in the Book of John. The other mention is in John 18:18 when Peter was standing and warming himself in front of a charcoal fire on the very spot where he denied the Lord three times.

Peter must have felt so wounded by denying the Lord that there were still lingering questions in his mind—doubts—that Jesus would ever really find favor with him again, as before.

Jesus knew this. Not long before, Peter had denied Jesus in front of a charcoal fire three times. Here, Jesus asked Peter if he loved him three times.

This time, Peter's responses were not anywhere near as confident as the night he adamantly assured Jesus that he would never deny him. That was the self-confident Peter. This was the broken Peter.

Even his responses to the "Do you love me?" questions were tepid. The word Jesus used for love was "agape," which means an unconditional, self-sacrificing love—the highest form of love. But Peter did not respond to Jesus in kind, using the same word for love as Jesus did. By the third time Jesus asked, Peter was grieved and said something more like, "Lord, you know all things. You know what I am capable of—you know my heart. You know that I can say that I am at least fond of you." Not a very rousing response.

Jesus wanted Peter to face his previous failure head-on. If he carried that wound around with him in the future, with all the associated guilt, he would never have been an effective witness for Christ. Jesus wanted Peter to move on in confidence, knowing that Jesus had known Peter's weakness all along; Peter just hadn't realized it.

It was never a matter of Peter showing Jesus his competence and courage, as he did when he cut off Malchus's ear in the Garden of Gethsemane. All along, Jesus was not looking for a hero, but just someone who loved him. Jesus is not in the business of dismissing people who fail or show weakness. He patiently waits for the right opportunity to use failure as a teachable moment when we can learn something about who he is and who we are, and then get up and get back into the game.

It was at this juncture that Jesus sent the self-sidelined Peter back to play ball: "Go tend my lambs and feed my sheep!" he said.

In the first chapter of John, Jesus began to gather his disciples—his sheep—and to feed them. The first question two of them asked him was, "Teacher, where are You staying?" His answer was, "Come, and you will see." So they followed him.

By the last chapter in the book we see Jesus commissioning Peter to do what Jesus did—to feed his lambs. By this time, the disciples knew where

Jesus was staying. He had come to stay inside of them. His final words to them then were the same as they were in the beginning, "Follow me!"

The other teachable moment in this story came after Jesus' dialogue with Peter. He had just finished telling Peter to "Follow me!" Peter then turned and saw John and asked the Lord, "What about this man?"

Jesus responded, "If I want him to remain until I come, what is that to you? You follow Me!"

Some of the disciples interpreted that to mean that John would never die. But that is not what Jesus meant.

What Jesus meant by that statement goes back to something that he had told his disciples while he was with them, before his crucifixion. He told them that within a generation—forty years—he would come again. It would be a coming in judgment on Jerusalem for having rejected him as their Messiah (Matthew 23-24). That happened in 70 A.D. All of those apostles—except John—died before that event took place. Only John survived to see it.

All of those apostles that were with Jesus from the beginning followed in the footsteps of their master, knowing rejection as he had, and a number of them died violent deaths, as he did.

The Bible is silent on exactly how each one died, but history and tradition give us some clues. In the decade before the fall of Jerusalem, the band of twelve began to split up and leave Jerusalem, going in different directions, taking the gospel to the ends of the earth.

According to tradition, along with some records from the Bible, eight of the apostles died as martyrs. At least two—Peter and Andrew—were crucified. Peter, according to tradition, was crucified upside down in Rome sometime in the mid 60s. John, the last living apostle, spent his remaining days in and around Ephesus (modern-day Turkey). Tradition tells us that he was thrown into a cauldron of boiling oil for his faith in Jesus, but miraculously escaped unharmed. His actual cause of death is unknown.

On the other side of the cross where self-confidence is dealt a stinging blow, there is grace, hope, and a commission of service for all of Jesus' disciples, including us. Though Jesus does come to live inside of us once we believe, he still needs to heal our wounds and transform our lives so that we will be made more like him and be able to serve others.

Just as God was able to use the cross as a tool in his hand for the disciples to learn humility, recognize their weaknesses, and understand that apart from him they could do nothing, he will help us learn these same lessons as well. In the end, our Jesus is not looking for heroes: the brave, the bold, or the confident who think they can do something great for God. Jesus is simply looking for those who humbly love him.

FINAL THOUGHTS

It has been a real joy and pleasure to share these "coffee sessions" with you. But it's time now for us to return to our daily lives.

I'd like to end with two final verses from the Book of John that I've referenced before and that come from the last two chapters. The first comes from the last chapter, last verse:

> And there were also many other things which Jesus did,
> which if they were written in detail, I suppose that even
> the world itself would not contain the books that would
> be written.
>
> JOHN 21:25

This book that you have just completed is only one more taking up space in an ever-expanding library that has the potential to exceed the boundaries of this planet. I do hope, however, that it has helped you in your understanding of the Book of John and that you have benefited and seen more of Jesus as a result of reading it.

Living with Jesus and knowing Jesus, John saw, heard, and experienced so much. Yet by comparison, he wrote so little. But what he did write was enough to fulfill his purpose for writing his book:

> Therefore many other signs Jesus also performed in the presence of the disciples, which are not written in this book; but these have been written so that you may believe that Jesus is the Christ, the Son of God; and that believing you may have life in His name.
>
> JOHN 20:30-31

For any seeker with an open heart, there is enough evidence presented in the Book of John to convince him or her that Jesus was the one sent from God, that he was the Son of God, and that by believing they will receive the eternal life that he has promised.

In conclusion, before we say goodbye, I'd like to wrap things up by passing on these final thoughts.

I'd like to call your attention back to our old friend Neo, from the Matrix. Remember that he started out seeking for truth. There was something inside of him that was not content living life as normal. He knew there was something more; he just didn't know where to find it.

But the truth came looking for him in the person of Morpheus. Morpheus had experienced life in a different realm, life that was real. He had experienced truth. He offered Neo a choice between a red pill and a blue pill.

Had Neo chosen the blue pill, life as he had known it would have continued with no significant change. He would have remained in a world of unreality, content to be living a lie, and he would never have known the life for which he was intended to live.

But once he did make the choice to take the red pill, his eyes were opened. From that point on, in order to realize his true identity, he had to reexamine everything he had perceived in the past to be the accepted reality.

By now, I hope you have been convinced that you were born into a world of pictures and shadows. There is a greater realm beyond that which we see with our eyes that needs to be discovered and explored. The spiritual reality presented in the Book of John is where truth resides, and knowing that truth will set you free.

Jesus is the truth. Jesus is what's real. And the purpose in this life for which you have been created is to know him!

Recall that once Neo took the red pill, he had to fight his battles in light of the new reality he had discovered. The same is true of us.

How do you fight?

The answer might sound alarmingly simple: You just need to believe. You fight by believing in Jesus, spending time with Jesus, loving Jesus, learning to abide in Jesus, and following Jesus.

How do you do that? I'll borrow from the slogan made famous by Nike: "Just Do It!"

Fortunately, you have not been left alone. You have a Helper living inside you whose job it is to lead you into all truth. You have Jesus living inside you. You have God living inside of you. That's quite a team. I think you are well equipped for the fight.

So, set as your goal to press on to know Jesus, who is the ultimate reality. I guarantee you that it will be worth it!

ACKNOWLEDGEMENTS

Thank you to Ric Peterson, Lance Thollander, and Jan Winterburn, long-time friends who walked through this book with me from beginning to end, contributing their spiritual insights, suggestions, and corrections. They served as the "John the Baptist forerunners" to help prepare this book enough to get it into the capable hands of Britta Eastburg Friesen (www.brittafriesen.com), the final editor. Britta put it all together and turned what seemed like a block of marble into something readable that resembles a work of art. It is my prayer that God will use this combined effort to speak into the hearts of many others and reveal more of Jesus Christ to them.

I'd also like to recognize Ed Miller (www.biblestudyministriesinc.net), a long-time Bible teacher, conference speaker, and friend, whose teachings I have grown and gleaned from over the years, and whose insights and revelations of Christ in the Scriptures have found their way into this book. Finally, I want to acknowledge the talented and artistic Sarah O'Neal who always comes through with the best of cover designs!

ABOUT THE AUTHOR

B O B   E M E R Y   is President and Founder of *Global Opportunities for Christ* (www.GOforChrist.org), a non-profit organization that supports indigenous Christian ministries around the world. For 10 years he ran a successful insurance and financial services business, which included the sales and marketing of insurance and investment products, mortgages, and trusts, as well as the recruiting, training, and managing of a substantial sales force.

In 1992 he left the business world to go into full-time missions work. In 1996 he founded *Global Opportunities for Christ* and has also served for 15 years as a missions consultant. Bob has traveled extensively overseas researching Christian ministries, cultivating relationships with Christian leaders, and teaching in churches, at conferences, and in Bible schools. He is the author of five books on various Christian topics.

HIS DESIRE IS FOR ME: *A 30-Day Devotional and Commentary on the Song of Songs*

Blending fiction, commentary, and thirty days of devotions, *His Desire Is for Me* provides daily, bite-sized portions of the Song of Songs for you to savor, meditate upon, and enjoy. It reveals the different stages believers go through on the road to spiritual maturity in their love for the Lord, from an initial love, to an increasing love, and finally unfolding into a mature love. Read it, and you will come to believe, with conviction, that his desire is truly for you!

— E D M I L L E R , Bible teacher and conference speaker:
"A commentary of commentaries on the Song of Songs."

THE NEW COVENANT

What is the New Covenant? What is the relationship between the Old Covenant and the New? Are both covenants still in effect? Does God still have a covenant relationship with Israel? Are there still Bible prophecies waiting to be fulfilled concerning the modern state of Israel and the rebuilding of a temple in Jerusalem before the Second Coming of Christ? How did the New

Testament come into being? How is the Lord's Supper to be celebrated, understood, and practiced? You will find answers to these questions and more in this New Testament trilogy under one cover featuring "The Messenger," "The Message," and "The Marriage" (which includes a dramatic commentary on the Book of Revelation). In *The New Covenant*, Bible commentary, doctrine, the prophetic word, the saga of the first century church, and New Testament principles all converge and come to life in one spellbinding story!

THE LORD'S SUPPER: *The Celebration of the New Covenant*

An excerpt from **THE NEW COVENANT**

For many, the true meaning of the Lord's Supper has been virtually lost. Draping it in layers of institutionalism, superstition, and religious attitudes borrowed from pagan religion, the enemy has done a masterful job of robbing Christians of their true inheritance in understanding the sacred significance of this simple transaction. In The Lord's Supper, these false layers are stripped away, revealing a joyful reality. Each time we partake of the bread and the cup, we are celebrating the Bible's overarching theme: our marriage relationship with our Lord Jesus. And that is truly something to celebrate!

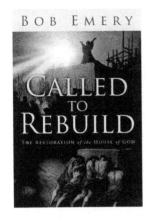

CALLED TO REBUILD: *The Restoration of the House of God*

This book is a commentary on Ezra and Nehemiah, along with the other "remnant books" of the Old Testament—Haggai, Zechariah, and Malachi. *Called to Rebuild* examines the historical and theological context of these post-exilic prophets and draws application for those who would be their spiritual descendants in this generation. This book is for those who have a heart to rebuild and see the church of today become all that God intended for it to be.

10830303R00187

Made in the USA
Monee, IL
03 September 2019